Language
and
Meaning

Papers from

The ASCD Tenth Curriculum Research Institute
Miami Beach, Florida, November 21-24, 1964
Detroit, Michigan, March 20-23, 1965

Edited by James B. Macdonald
Director of the Institute Staff

and

Robert R. Leeper
Editor, ASCD Publications

Association for Supervision and Curriculum Development, NEA
1201 Sixteenth Street, N.W., Washington, D. C. 20036

Contents

Mary Jane McCue Aschner
Associate Professor of Education, Boston University, Massachusetts

Thomas J. Johnson
Assistant Professor of Educational Psychology, University of Wisconsin, Madison

Foreword

THROUGH its publications, commissions, committees, and its national conference, the Association for Supervision and Curriculum Development has constantly sought to reduce the gap between new understandings arising in the scholarly disciplines and their implementation in the practices of education. As part of this program it has offered through its Research Commission, in cooperation with the National Institute of Mental Health, a series of research institutes in various parts of the country devoted to the exploration of new ideas from the learned arts and sciences and the stimulation and design of research in many phases of educational thought and practice. To do this they have sought the assistance of a distinguished list of scholars from psychiatry, psychology, anthropology, economics, sociology, philosophy, medicine and the various branches of the physical sciences. The papers presented in this booklet are in that tradition.

Tremendous efforts are currently being aimed at producing change in the curriculum through manipulation of content and subject matter, by shifting patterns of school and classroom organization, by electronic and mechanical gadgets or simply by increasing the output expected of students and teachers everywhere. In the midst of all this activity the Tenth ASCD Curriculum Research Institute deliberately planned to devote its attention to the problems of language and meaning. The choice seems especially appropriate in these times when many educators are deeply concerned that the human aspects of schooling are often neglected. Language, after all, is the vehicle by which most teaching is accomplished. Meaning is the human goal of learning, the ultimate test of any curriculum change.

To set the stage for the discussions in this institute a group of eminent scholars was invited to share their thinking with the institute members. Following this the participants spent several days in lively discussion on the implications of these questions for our public schools. Unfortunately, we cannot share in all those discussions. It is a privilege, however, for ASCD to publish the papers of the distinguished consultants who spoke at the institute and so to make these available to the profession. The papers from previous institutes have also been published by ASCD and are available from the Association's headquarters in Washington.

April 1966   ARTHUR W. COMBS, *President*
                                                 Association for Supervision
                                              and Curriculum Development

Acknowledgments

Final editing of the manuscript and production of this booklet were the responsibility of Robert R. Leeper, Associate Secretary and Editor, ASCD Publications. Technical production was handled by Mary Ann Lurch, Editorial Assistant, assisted by Teola T. Jones, Staff Assistant, under the general supervision of Ruth P. Ely, Editorial Associate.

Language, Meaning and Motivation: An Introduction

James B. Macdonald

NECESSITY can be both the father of innovation and the hand-maiden of disaster. Any administrator could tell us, with a little re-flection on his part, that the pressure of decision can spur one on to new insights or encourage one to seek simple solutions for complex problems. The pressures on our educational system today have produced the necessity for change and consequently an unparalleled chance for progress or disastrous error.

The direction and format for change are becoming clearer each year. The direction of change is toward increasing use of technology and automation in education and the critical revision and reformulation of subject matter. The format for change is increasingly toward central-ized direction in the hands of an oligarchy of scholars and bureaucrats buttressed by the immense expenditures of federal monies for centrally selected purposes.

We are riding a crest of a wave of socially expedient reform in education rather than reform emerging in light of the historical perspec-tive of curriculum development. The changes themselves may be poten-tially reasonable but the method of bringing them about has faced the educator with some of the realities of living which he either chooses to ignore or has been too naive to recognize before this time.

It is interesting to note that the prominent critics have selected John Dewey and Progressive Education as their antithesis. There is some reason to doubt the acuity of their awareness of Dewey and the Prag-matic philosophy he espoused. The critics in essence believe in the same central idea of progress brought about by rational problem solv-ing, and apparently the collateral idea that the worth of their doing

1

lies in the consequences of their actions, although they have not shown much interest in empirically evaluating their projected consequences (see, e.g., [1]).

Structure of the Disciplines Approach

There is at this time no basis for seeing current curriculum reform as progress or disaster; however, already some doubts are beginning to form. What was accepted uncritically as the need of our society to upgrade education through discussion and description of the structure of each discipline, is not clearly as useful as it was first thought to be (see, e.g., [2]).

Indeed one might say that the scholars have perpetrated and projected an experiment upon the schools. Their efforts are witness to at least as much faith that structures and modes of inquiry exist, as they are evidence of some sort of access to knowledge that ordinary mortals do not possess.

The scholars, of course, speak from strength and authority. When they tell us there is a structure of a discipline and a mode (or modes) of inquiry, they appeal to experience beyond our own ability to validate. Thus, we must accept their statements upon faith in their authority. Yet the results are not impressive. Some few scholars (see, e.g., [3]) say the whole movement is hogwash, and other scholars (especially in the social sciences) have not been able to produce much in the way of structures.

From another viewpoint the scholars' behavior could almost be said to be irresponsible. It is at least *possible* that it would have been more useful in the long run if scholars had reorganized their own material for courses at the college level and tried it out with their own students before they moved so definitely into other levels of the curriculum. Public education is providing them with an opportunity to learn a great deal at the expense of others.

The universities, with rare exceptions, have infrequently shown any desire or ability to bring about curriculum change in their own settings. They are wedded to the concept of academic freedom in which they apparently see no corollary at lower levels. Is it all a matter of degree or a difference in kind? Does the university professor (or his graduate assistant) know so much that no syllabus or course of study is necessary for him in contrast to the public school teacher? Charity begins at home and the college student is suffering ills that need the expert attention of the scholar.

Perhaps the most difficult thing to understand is the apparent lack of comprehension by the scholars of the history of curriculum in the 20th century. The outcome of the Woods Hole Conference, for example, popularized by Jerome S. Bruner in *The Process of Education,* makes no reference to Alfred North Whitehead's (4) or Charles Judd's (5) statements early in the century about "structure" of the disciplines. Even attempts to organize social studies around the basic generalizations in the area, found in the 1920s (6), are never mentioned. In all, the performance has been a very unscholarly one on the part of scholars.

What assurance is there that the new movement in any way evades the criticism of the old subject matter curriculum? Curriculum, all dressed up in its new suit may well appear to the child much like the emperor's clothes. Public school people may perhaps have been seduced into thinking the emperor has a new suit.

There is, indeed, nothing in recent curriculum development which alters in any fundamental way the historically available thought in the field of curriculum. Indeed, there is much in the present process and direction of change that violates long lasting values and/or developmental procedures that have been hard won from experience over the years. This being the case perhaps a reminder of the larger context and meaning of education is in order.

Beyond Formal Knowledge

There is a deeper and broader reality than the substance of our communications to one another. Somehow the rationally intended and agreed upon messages we send and receive, interpret and respond to are a crucial but partial part of our meaning structure. Deeper than the formally structured concepts, ideas or insights are the very meanings inherent in the structure of language; and broader than these same ideas are the personal connotations, motivations and desires that make them relevant.

It is senseless and stupid to quarrel with the suggestion that we ought to know what we know in a formal and organized sense. Thus, the structure of a discipline can be a useful pedagogical tool. Still, better organizing schemes for knowledge cannot replace the function of language itself, or breathe life for the individual into the essential "outthereness" of culturally accumulated knowledge.

Indeed, schools must have both a pedagogically packaged cultural heritage and the means for bringing to life and for understanding the deeper meanings of individual and cultural existence which pervade learning in the experiences of persons.

The past few years have revealed an increasing growth in societies' concern for the forms of knowledge. We have moved a great distance from what our critics might call a lack of concern for the functions of knowledge. Frequently this dichotomy has been posed in the terms "content" versus "process." Yet the dichotomy is just that—a dichotomy— and the two, form and function, are so intertwined that they cannot be viewed as mutually exclusive terms.

Attempts to substitute a new process have been proposed under the aegis of "modes of inquiry." By this proposal the dichotomy is hopefully resolved into the formal areas of knowledge, and *concepts* become one side of the coin, *inquiry processes* the other side.

If this is indeed true, then we need a three-legged stool for analogy rather than a two-sided coin; for a third element—*personal meaning*— must still be involved.

The present concern for the disciplines, their structure and modes of inquiry, reflects a social theory of knowledge (see, e.g., [7]). Thus, knowledge is formed for its social uses and discovered or invented as a result of social stimulation. Groups of scholars can be and are sub-systems of society with their own status and roles, prestige and reward systems. Knowledge is created for the use of the scholar in this erudite but not less social system. This created knowledge can then be made available for the broader society in applied packages of a variety of sorts.

The broader and deeper meanings of knowledge go beyond a contemporary societal view and reflect cultural and personal theories of knowledge. A functional conceptualization of culture would suggest the development of a social theory of knowledge which "fits" our culture. The very fact that ours is a "scientific" culture, at least in some sense, may be related to the broader cultural values found in our society; and, at the root of this rests the cause-effect thinking inherent in our subject-predicate language forms. Thus, the "structure of our disciplines" and the "modes of our inquiry" are as surely grounded in a selected set of cultural values, of which they represent one set of alternatives, as any other select phenomena of language.

Personal knowledge brings depth to meaning and reflects the uniqueness of our own experiences.The connotation we bring to words, the commitments we give to certain ideas, or the perceptual selections we make from among relevant alternatives are all predicated upon and integrated through the unique being of each individual.

Reid (8) phrases the personal aspect of knowledge succinctly. He says:

Yet, without denying at all the absolutely crucial importance of symbolic statement of different kinds for the growth and development of human understanding, one can also say that knowledge, although partly expressed in statements, never *consists* of the statements; and the living mind is always much more than can be contained in any number of statements.

Gaining knowledge, then, is not quite the simple matter of mastering man's statements about reality, no matter how well organized these statements may be for pedagogical purposes and social uses. The very forms of man's symbols are creations of the culture in which he lives and predispose him to limit and shape his awareness of the "to be known" in the forms of his symbolic structures. Yet the abstracting of experience through symbolic form does not encompass all of what is to be known with reference to the statements of reality, nor does it preclude the necessity of knowledge being possessed by a living person.

Focus of the Institutes

Sometimes the ferment which stirs a new "untidy" life in a pupil's mind is much more valuable than the assimilation and tidy reproduction of statements given to him. It is doubtful whether by present standards we do justice to this. The concepts of "knowledge" and "knowing" need attention. There is a tendency among scientists and philosophers—and educationists influenced by them—to "corner" the word "knowledge" and exploit it for important but limited ends. The ordinary uses of the word are much more liberal. Reflection upon the more liberal uses may liberalize the concept of the increase of "knowledge" which we seek when we educate (9).

It was the very hope of the Curriculum Research Institutes that the presentations of the invited speakers would provide a fresh impetus to review the perspective of a broader and deeper meaning of knowledge and refocus educators upon the more liberal uses of the concept.

There is no intention here to reject the social uses of knowledge, but primarily to temper the present resurgence of structures and modes, big ideas and logical strategies, with the heat of perspective.

There is, after all, no reason to suspect that the reformulation of content alone in the schools will suffice to counter the loss of self, the dehumanization and depersonalization of people living in a technological society such as ours. Further, there is no reason to suspect that the structure of the disciplines can by magic of the reorganization reduce the threat of nuclear holocaust, bring justice and equality to all peoples, or provide a basis for freedom from poverty for all.

No one, to be sure, has made such claims, but we might pause to ask why the climate of our time makes education "ripe" for this epistemological recipe. Is this phenomenon another example of rationalizing rationality? Could this movement be related to the overall technological trend to systematize all human interaction? Is this primarily a project of human engineering based upon an efficiency motif?

Perhaps only time will tell. However, it will do no harm and may promise some good to stretch the rubber band of educational thought a bit to include a clearer understanding of language, meaning and motivation within the knowledge package.

Relationships of the Papers to the Theme

The concepts of language, meaning and motivation encompass a phenomenally wide variety of potential topics. The papers presented here only make a small offering to the altar of the intellect in these areas. Yet perusal of these statements should prove to be challenging and productive of exciting ideas for most readers.

Dwayne Huebner brings the discipline of commitment and historical perspective to the problems of curriculum conceptualizations. His search among the broader aspects of our culture for old and new ways to talk about curriculum provides a much needed "set" for viewing the curriculum scene.

Philip H. Phenix supplies the framework of analytic philosophy to the problems of knowledge in the curriculum. His refusal to lose sight of the contextual elements of our knowledge statements is impressive both in its exhibition of scholarly discipline and in the insights it can stimulate for curriculum developers.

The element of felt meaning is deftly probed by Eugene T. Gendlin. His journey takes us into the reaches of the unstatable but knowable interplay of affect and cognition in human activity. From the perspective of the clinical psychologist, he clearly exposes the depth of personal knowing in a stimulating and suggestive manner.

Aspects of the potential multi-faceted meanings of language are discussed by Walter Loban. His lucid and fast moving statements about what language reveals about people and itself; and the problems and prospects of teaching people to use language effectively reflect the curiosity, concern and understanding which have grown out of years of research in the area of children's language learning.

Mary Jane McCue Aschner's distinction between "attached" and "addressed" meanings and their relationship to thinking is fruitfully descriptive of important understandings. Her discussion of three conceptions of thinking in classroom research provides an interesting setting for the development of suggestions for the design of curriculum tasks. The final paper deals with motivation. Thomas J. Johnson brings the skill and perspective of the experimental psychologist to one of the most perplexing areas of psychology. His review of motivation theory, and his description of his own unusually imaginative research is impressive, refreshing and promising.

In all, then, the papers in this publication provide a wide and varied display of special interests and perspectives on the topic of the Curriculum Research Institutes. They are dedicated in patterned essence, if not in specific intent, to a broader and deeper awareness of the problems and insights concerning knowledge of and in the curriculum. To this extent one may feel confident they have succeeded with a flourish.

References

1. Jerome S. Bruner. "Education as Social Invention." *Saturday Review,* Educational Supplement 44 (8): 70-103; February 19, 1966.

2. Herbert M. Kliebard. "Structure of the Disciplines as an Educational Slogan." *Teachers College Record* 66 (7): 598-603; April 1965.

3. Alexander Calandra. "The New Science Curriculum: A Sharp Dissent." *School Management* 8 (11): 76-82; 1964.

4. Alfred North Whitehead. *The Aims of Education.* New York: A Mentor Book, The New American Library, 1949.

5. Charles H. Judd. *Education as Cultivation of the Higher Mental Process.* New York: The Macmillan Company, 1955.

6. Neal Billings. *A Determination of Generalizations Basic to the Social Studies Curriculum.* Baltimore: Warwick and York, 1929.

7. Michael Polanyi. "The Republic of Science, Its Political and Economic Theory." *Minerva* 1 (1): 54-73; Autumn 1962.

8. L. A. Reid. *Philosophy and Education.* New York: International Publication Service, 1962. p. 34-35.

9. *Ibid.,* p. 35.

Curricular Language and
Classroom Meanings

Dwayne Huebner

THE educator participates in the paradoxical structure of the universe. He wishes to talk about language, but must use language for his talk. He infers that meanings exist, but has only language, or other symbol systems, as a vehicle for his inference. Hemmed in by his language, he nevertheless has audacity to tackle problems on the edge of his awareness. The educator would talk of the language of children? With what language would he do this? Would he identify the meanings significant for young people? What meanings, shaped by what language, give him the power to do so? It is as if he detected a speck in his student's eye, but failed to notice the log in his own.

Release from the confinement of existing language, or more appropriately, transcendence of existing patterns of speech is available through several channels. The theologian would argue that the vicious circle is broken or transcended only by grace, mediated through the openness and receptivity available through prayer. The aesthetician would argue that literature, specifically poetry, enables lowly man to break out of his verbal prison and to achieve "a victory over language."[1] The scientist would point to his success with observation, classification, hypothesis formation, and experimentation as a way of breaking through language barriers. The critic of social ideologies would argue that "conventional wisdom"[2] is destroyed and reformed only by the "massive onslaught of circumstance with which they cannot contend."[3]

[1] John Middleton Murry. *The Problem of Style.* London: Oxford University Press, 1922. p. 101.

[2] John Kenneth Galbraith. *The Affluent Society.* Boston: Houghton Mifflin Company, 1958. p. 9.

[3] *Ibid.,* p. 20.

Unfortunately, the language which shapes the thought of the curricular specialist is not usually part of prayerful acts, nor can the educator depend upon revelation or prophecy to refresh and recondition his language. If grace operates in the educational realm, it does so through other channels. Likewise, curricular language is, again unfortunately, not within the realm of literature. The formulator and writer of curricular language is seldom an artist. The penetrating image or significant metaphor is infrequently found in pedagogical materials. This misfortune is intensified by the nearsightedness of the educator who tries to be scientific by throwing out subjective formulations, yet who never quite produces a language system which can be made, shattered and reconstituted through the creative methodologies of science.

The curricular worker is stuck, so to speak, with conventional wisdom, which yields only to the "onslaught of circumstance." The onslaught of educational circumstances is felt differently by various educators. The individual educator's professional sensory and cognitive system is a delicate instrument for detecting shifts in his educational world. His responsiveness takes the form of new actions and new speech. Fortunately, all educators have not been shaped by the same conditioning agents, their sensory and cognitive systems detect different shifts, and their responsiveness takes different forms. Who knows, from such chaos a science might emerge! Given sufficient grace, the educator might even be blessed with the highest possible form of human creation—poetic wisdom.

Today's curricular language seems filled with dangerous, non-recognized myths; dangerous not because they are myths, but because they remain non-recognized and unchallenged. The educator accepts as given the language which has been passed down to him by his historical colleagues. He forgets that language was formed by man, for his purposes, out of his experiences—not by God with ultimate truth value. As a product of the educator's past and as a tool for his present, current curricular language must be put to the test of explaining existing phenomena and predicting or controlling future phenomena. Such curricular language must be continually questioned, its effectiveness challenged, its inconsistencies pointed out, its flaws exposed, and its presumed beauty denied. It must be doubted constantly, yet used humbly, with the recognition that that is all he has today. Perhaps tomorrow the educator will have better language, if he stays open to the world which speaks to him, and responds with the leap of the scientist, or the vision of the poet.

Myths in Curricular Language

Two tyrannical myths are embedded deeply in curricular language. One is that of learning—the other that of purpose. These have become almost magical elements within curricular language. The curricular worker is afraid to ignore them, let alone question them, for fear of the wrath of the gods. Fortunately, curricular language is not basically a ritualistic form, although incantations are frequently offered in the educational temples identified as college classrooms and in sacramental gatherings called faculty meetings. The roof will not fall in if these elements are deprecated and partially ignored. A talisman need not be rubbed if one acknowledges that learning is merely a postulated concept, not a reality; and that goals and objectives are not always needed for educational planning.

Indeed, curricular language seems rather ludicrous when the complexity and the mystery of a fellow human being is encompassed in that technical term of control—the "learner." Think of it—there standing before the educator is a being partially hidden in the cloud of unknowing. For centuries the poet has sung of his near infinitudes; the theologian has preached of his depravity and hinted of his participation in the divine; the philosopher has struggled to encompass him in his systems, only to have him repeatedly escape; the novelist and dramatist have captured his fleeting moments of pain and purity in never-to-be-forgotten aesthetic forms; and the man engaged in curriculum has the temerity to reduce this being to a single term—"learner." E. E. Cummings speaks with greater force to the same point.[4]

> O sweet spontaneous
> earth how often have
> the
> doting
>
>   fingers of
> prurient philosophers pinched
> and
> poked
>
> thee
> , has the naughty thumb
> of science prodded
> thy

[4] Copyright, 1923, 1951, by E. E. Cummings. Reprinted from his volume *Poems 1923-1954* by permission of Harcourt, Brace & World, Inc.

beauty   . how
often have religions taken
thee upon their scraggy knees
squeezing and

buffeting thee that thou mightest conceive
gods
        (but
true

to the incomparable
couch of death thy
rhythmic
lover

    thou answerest

    them only with

        spring)

The educator confronts the human being and no language will ever do him in or do him justice. Yet the curricular worker seems unwilling to deal with mystery or doubt or unknowables. Mysteries are reduced to problems, doubts to error, and unknowables to yet-to-be-discoverables. The curriculum worker cannot deal with these because his language is selected from the symbol systems of the social scientists and psychologists—whereas mysteries, doubts and unknowns are better handled by poetry, philosophy and religion. His language, his pedaguese, hides the mysteries, doubts and unknowns from him. Likewise, he assumes that all human behavior is caused or has purpose, and that consequently his educational activities must be goal-oriented. This leads, at times, to ignoring the fullness of the eternal present for the sterility of the known future. This has also led to the continual discussion of educational purpose as if such discussion is the only valid entrance into the curricular domain.

As with any myth, there is sufficient truth or value in these concepts of learning and goals or purpose, and the language which supports them, to warrant their continual use in curriculum. However, to the extent that these notions are tyrannical and prevent the development of other forms of curricular thought, they serve demonic forces. No language system is so good or significant that other language systems cannot eventually take its place—unless it is an aesthetic form. But an aesthetic form has no instrumental value. Other conceptual models *are* possible for curricular problems and phenomena, and concepts which inhibit their development must sometimes be violently uprooted in order that the phenomena of concern can be more clearly seen.

Traditional Curricular Tasks

More or less traditional curricular thought, at least since Tyler,[5] has operated with four basic problems or tasks: the formulation of educational "objectives," the selection of "learning" experiences, the organization of those learning experiences and their evaluation. Other curricular writers expand or add to these four, but the basic framework does not change. Here tyrannical mythology is freely displayed. The title is "The Organization of Learning Experiences." Why not the organization of educational experiences? The formulation of objectives is the first step; necessary, incidentally, because evaluation is the final step. With these objectives, experiences can be selected, organized, and evaluated. By framing curricular tasks in this language, the curricular worker is immediately locked into a language system which determines his questions as well as his answers.

To break from this framework, the language of learning and purpose must be cast aside and new questions asked. To do this the curricular worker must confront his reality directly, not through the cognitive spectacles of a particular language system. As he does this, he is then forced to ask, "What language or language system can be used to talk about these phenomena?" His reality must be accepted, not his language; for many language systems may be used for a given reality.

The two major realities which confront the curricular worker are the activities within a classroom, or activities designated in other ways as educational, and the existential situation of choice among differing classroom activities. This is an oversimplification, of course, for the educator's primary dimension of existence is time, rather than space, and the temporal nature of these realities is ignored for this analysis.

Educational Realities

The first reality is that of educational activity. What is and what is not educational activity becomes, at the extremes, a category problem,

5 Ralph W. Tyler. "The Organization of Learning Experiences." In: *Toward Improved Curriculum Theory.* Virgil Herrick and Ralph Tyler, editors. Chicago: University of Chicago Press, 1950. p. 59-67.

but generally educators can walk from one classroom or school to another and point out to a non-educator what they consider to be educational activity. Furthermore, they can dream about the future and envisage educational activity in certain places or among certain people. The language problem which emerges when the educator confronts this educational activity, his first reality, is how to talk about it or how to describe it. How does the teacher talk about his instruction as he plans it or as he describes it to another? How does the supervisor describe the classroom situation as he seeks to help the teacher? How does the curriculum planner talk about events which he wants to happen in classrooms?How does the teacher educator discuss classroom phenomena with his students? How does the researcher describe the classroom events that he studies?

The power of curricular mythologies becomes visible when the problem is posed this way, for the educator is apt to describe the student as a learner, the teacher becomes a goal setter, or a reinforcing agent. Classroom activity is seen as a learning process in action, and indeed teaching is often seen as the mirror image of learning. This problem of description of educational activity has been solved in many ways. Most methods books have some kind of solution. The studies of teaching by Hughes,[6] Smith,[6] Aschner,[6] Bellack,[7] and many others are all efforts to develop a language which can be used to describe classroom action. Teachers have their own way of talking and thinking about what they are doing in the classroom. Many of the studies of newer curricula are descriptions of what teachers can do in the classroom with students. This descriptive problem is both a scientific problem and an aesthetic one,[8] for it is at the level of description that science and poetry can merge.

The first reality is also related to a second problem—that of choice among viable alternatives. Selection among alternatives requires some form of valuing, or at least some hierarchy of values. The second language problem becomes that of making conscious or explicit the value framework. When values are explicated a rationality is produced which enables the maximizing of that value. In turn, this rationality contains descriptive terminology which may be used to solve the first

[6] Arno Bellack. *Theory and Research in Teaching.* New York: Bureau of Publications, Teachers College, Columbia University, 1963.

[7] Arno Bellack. *The Language of the Classroom.* New York: The Institute of Psychological Research, Teachers College, Columbia University, 1963.

[8] F. S. C. Northrup. *The Logic of the Sciences and the Humanities.* New York: The Macmillan Company, 1947. p. 169-90.

problem. The valuing problem and the description problem are consequently intertwined, thus complicating curricular language.

The key curricular questions, rather neutral from most descriptive and value points of view, are "What can go on in the classroom?" and "How can this activity be valued?" The central notion of curricular thought can be that of "valued activity." All curricular workers attempt to identify and/or develop "valued educational activity." The most effective move from this central notion is the clarification of the value frameworks or systems which may be used to value educational activity.

Value Systems

Five value frameworks or systems may be identified. The terms which identify them are not as precise as they might be, but discussion and criticism should aid in sharpening them. For purposes of discussion, and eventually criticism, they may be labeled *technical, political, scientific, aesthetic* and *ethical* values.

Technical

Current curricular ideology reflects, almost completely, a technical value system. It has a means-ends rationality that approaches an economic model. End states, end products, or objectives are specified as carefully and as accurately as possible, hopefully in behavioral terms. Activities are then designed which become the means to these ends or objectives. The primary language systems of legitimation and control are psychological and sociological languages. Ends or objectives are identified by a sociological analysis of the individual in the present or future social order, and these ends or objectives are then translated into psychological language—usually in terms of concepts, skills, attitudes or other behavioral terms. With these ends clearly in mind the language of psychology, primarily of learning, is used to generate, or at least sanction, certain activities which can produce these defined ends.

Major concerns for the curricular worker are the mobilization of material and human resources to produce these ends. Books and audio-visual or other sensory aids are brought to the students, or students are taken to actual phenomena. Teachers are trained, hired or placed to produce the right mixture of human and material resources. Organization, and, to an extent not readily recognized in curricular thought, costs are carefully scrutinized and some effort at efficiency is made. The control of the input of materials and human resources is a major source of control of this means-ends system. Evaluation, from the point of view of the technical value system, may be considered a type of quality control. The end product is scrutinized to see if it can go on the market with the stamp of approval, or if not yet at the end of the production line, the inadequate products-in-process are shunted aside to be reworked by remedial efforts until they can return to the normal production line. Evaluation, or inspection, also serves to check the quality of activities in the producing sequence. These activities may be improved or altered if the end states are not what they should be.

Technical valuing and economic rationality are valid and necessary modes of thought in curriculum. The school does serve a technical function in society by conserving, developing and increasing human resources which are essential for the maintenance and improvement of the society. This technical function is obvious during wartime, when schools and universities are taken over to serve national purposes. During peacetime, the same social needs exist, but the technical values and economic rationality are apt to be hidden behind the verbal cloaks which a democratic society wraps around itself. So the educator talks of the need for individuals to read, to write, to compute, to think in certain ways, and to make a living in order to exist productively in his society. Technical valuing and economic rationality are necessary in curricular thought, for problems of scarcity and of institutional purpose do exist. However, this is but one value system among five, and to reduce all curricular thought to this one is to weaken the educator's power and to pull him out of the mysteriously complex phenomena of human life.

Political

The second category, political valuing, also exists in curricular thought; more often covertly than overtly. This value category exists because the teacher, or other educator, has a position of power and control. He influences others directly or through the manipulation of resources. To remain in a position of effective power, he must seek the support of those in positions to reward him or influence his behavior in some way. His work, his teaching or educational leadership, becomes the vehicle by which people judge the worth of his influence and hence decide whether he is worthy of their support, respect, or positive sanctions. Educational activity is consequently valued by the teacher, or other curricular leader, for the support or respect that it brings him.

The teacher acts in ways that bring positive support from the principal, superintendent, parents, colleagues, or college professors. Merit ratings, promotions, positions of responsibility, respect in the community, informal leadership among staff members are all fruits of acceptable and enviable efforts. The teacher may produce classroom activity which pleases the custodian, thus assuring him of a quick response when the room needs special attention or when supplies are needed. The superintendent may act to create classroom activity which brings forth rave notices from critical reporters, or accolades from university professors, thus gaining him more prestige in the community. He may need to act in certain ways, to influence classroom activities, in order to gain maximum support for the next bond issue.

The search for increased recognition or power is not inherently bad. A teacher or educational leader must have minimal power to influence others. His efforts are apt to be more successful if he has this power, or at least the trust and respect of those who count. The rationality that accompanies this form of valuing is a political rationality, in which the curricular worker seeks to maximize his power or prestige in order that he may accomplish his work as effectively as possible.

All educational activity is valued politically. The teacher who claims to be immune is so only because he is in equilibrium with his educational community. But given a change of situation, administrators, lay attitudes, or colleagues, that one-time non-politically oriented teacher must again rethink how his educational activity reflects upon his standing in the local educational community. There is nothing evil or immoral about political rationality and valuing. Indeed it is necessary if personal influence and responsibility are to be maximized. Of course, if power and prestige are sought as ends, rather than as means for responsible and creative influence, evil and immorality may be produced. Yet dreams and visions are not realized without personal or professional power. Hannah Arendt, in her *Human Condition*, identifies politics as one of the great arts of man, a fact too often forgotten in this day of self-aggrandizement and materialism.

Scientific

Scientific activity may be broadly designated as that activity which produces new knowledge with an empirical basis. Hence educational activity may be valued for the knowledge that it produces about that activity. The teacher, the curricular worker, the educational researcher are always in need of more and better warranted assertions about educational activity. They can construct and manipulate teaching situations to test new hypotheses, or to produce new facts as new technologies and techniques are introduced. Whereas technical valuing seeks to maximize change in students, scientific valuing seeks to maximize the attainment of information or knowledge for the teacher or educator.

The rationality by which scientific values are heightened is some form of scientific methodology. This methodology may take the form of action research or of controlled experimental design. It may be nothing more than exposing students to new situations and ordering the forthcoming responses. Teachers may seek to create unique classroom situations which will give them more information about individual students. Researchers may expose children to new teaching strategies in order to discover necessary conditions for the use of given materials or the accomplishment of certain ends. A total packaged curriculum may be tested to produce information about how teachers and students respond to a given curriculum.

Scientific valuing is a necessary form of curricular valuing. Only as new facts are produced and as new assertions are warranted can the educational enterprise keep pace with the world of which it is a part. Only as individual teachers seek more precise knowledge about their students and about their teaching procedures can they stay abreast of the "onslaught of circumstance." Educational activity valued only for the change produced in students or for the support it brings to teachers is narrowly conceived, for it may also produce significant changes in the educator if he undertakes it with the sensitivities of the scientist.

Aesthetic

The aesthetic valuing of educational activity is often completely ignored, perhaps because the educator is not sufficiently concerned with or knowledgeable about aesthetic values or perhaps because aesthetic activities are not highly prized today in society. Scientific and technical values are more highly prized consciously, and political values are more highly prized unconsciously or covertly. Valued aesthetically, educational activity would be viewed as having symbolic and aesthetic meanings. At least three dimensions of this value category may be identified.

First is what Bullough calls the element of psychical distance.[9] The aesthetic object, in this case educational activity, is removed from

---

[9] Edward Bullough. "Psychical Distance as a Factor in Art and an Esthetic Principle." In: *A Modern Book of Aesthetics*. Melvin Rader, editor. New York: Henry Holt and Company, 1952.

the world of use. It is a conditioned object which does not partake of the conditioned world; that is, it has no use, no functional or instrumental significance, and consequently may partake of or be symbolic of the unconditional. It is possibility realized, ordinarily impossible in the functional world. It is spontaneity captured, normally lost in the ongoing world. Because of aesthetic distance, the art object, in this case educational activity, is the possibility of life, captured and heightened and standing apart from the world of production, consumption and intent. The art object has beauty. Educational activity can have beauty.

The second dimension of the aesthetic category is that of wholeness and design. Because the aesthetic object stands outside of the functional world it has a totality and unity which can be judged or criticized. The art critic speaks of balance, of harmony, of composition, of design, of integration and of closure. The art object may be a source of contentment and peace, of a unity to be found only in the realm of perfection, the land of dreaming innocence. Educational activity may thus be valued in terms of its sense of wholeness, of balance, of design and of integrity, and its sense of peace or contentment.

The third dimension of aesthetic value is that of symbolic meaning. Any aesthetic object is symbolic of man's meanings. It reflects the meanings of the artist as an individual; it also reflects the meaning existing in and emerging from man as a life form. The aesthetic object, indeed educational activity, may be valued for the meanings that it reveals, and may be valued for its truth. Educational activity is symbolic of the meanings of the educator, as an individual and as a spokesman for man. The teaching of educators who are spiteful, unrealized human beings reflects these inner meanings. The meaninglessness and routine of much educational activity today reflects the meaninglessness and routine of a mechanistic world order. In the rare classroom is the possible vitality and significance of life symbolized by the excitement, fervor and community of educational activity. Educational activity can symbolize the meanings felt and lived by educators.

Ethical

Finally, educational activity may be valued for its ethical values. Here the educational activity is viewed primarily as an encounter between man and man, and as ethical categories for valuing this encounter come into being, Metaphysical and perhaps religious language become the primary vehicle for the legitimation and thinking through of educational activity. The concern in this value category is not on the significance of the educational act for other ends, or the realization of other values, but the value of the educational act per se.

For some, the encounter of man with man is seen as the essence of life, and the form that this encounter takes is the meaning of life. The encounter is not *used* to produce change, to enhance prestige, to identify new knowledge, or to be symbolic of something else. The encounter *is*. In it is the essence of life. In it life is revealed and lived. The student is not viewed as an object, an *it;* but as a fellow human being, another subject, a *thou,* who is to be lived with in the fullness of the present moment or the eternal present. From the ethical stance the educator meets the student, not as an embodied role, as a lesser category, but as a fellow human being who demands to be accepted on the basis of fraternity not simply on the basis of equality. No thing, no conceptual barrier, no purpose intrudes between educator and student when educational activity is valued ethically. The fullness of the educational activity, as students encounter each other, the world around them, and the teacher, is all there is. The educational activity is life— and life's meanings are witnessed and lived in the classroom.

Educational activity is seldom, if ever, valued from within only one of the value categories. Rather all five are, or may be, brought to bear in the valuing process. Today, classroom activity is viewed primarily from the technological value category, but political considerations are also brought to bear; and scientific, aesthetic, and ethical values may be brought to bear. The proposition may be put forth that educational activity in classrooms will be richer and more meaningful if all five categories are brought to bear. Indeed, the insignificance and inferior quality of much teaching today may be a result of attempts to maximize only the technical and political and perhaps scientific values without adequate attention to the aesthetic and ethical values. Classroom activity which is socially significant because of heightened technical efficiency might have greater personal significance for students and teacher if the aesthetic and ethical categories were also used to value the activity. But these notions become possibilities for further search and eventually research.

Systems of Rationality

Curricular language is not simple. Many ways can be found or utilized to identify and choose "valued educational activity." The five value categories which have been proposed carry with them forms of rationality which may be used to talk about classroom activity. These forms of rationality are not adequately developed here, and require much more effort before they can be used to analyze, describe, or create educational activity. However, the general aspects are perhaps sufficiently developed to explore the dimensions of classroom meanings which may exist. Attention will be given to ethical and aesthetic valuing and possible forms of rationality which may accompany them. The technical is well represented in current curricular literature. The scientific and political are hinted at in a few places, although specific curricular implications need to be developed.

Ethical Rationality

Ethical valuing demands that the human situation existing between student and teacher must be uppermost, and that content must be seen as an arena of that human confrontation. This human situation must be picked away at until the layers of the known are peeled back and the unknown in all of its mystery and awe strikes the educator in the face and heart, and he is left with the brute fact that he is but a man trying to influence another man. A man is being influenced, even if in the form of a child. And it is another man who is influencing, somehow daring to make judgments, to direct attention, to impose demands, and to recommend action and thoughts. How dare he so dare? Probably because he is aware that he has, as have all beings, the power to influence.

Awareness of the power to influence may lead to hubris, the demonic state of false pride in the educator's own omnipotence, or to the humbling recognition that with the power to influence comes the life-giving possibility of being influenced. The humble acceptance of his power to influence and to be influenced makes possible his freedom to promise and forgive and his willingness to do so. An act of education is an act of influence: one man trying to influence another man. Educational activity is ethical when the educator recognizes that he participates in this human situation of mutual influence, and when he accepts his ability to promise and to forgive.

The educational activity differs from other human encounters by this emphasis on influence, for clearly the educator is seen, and accepted, as a person who legitimately attempts to influence. However, he operates within the uniquely human endeavor of conversation, the giving and receiving of the word at the frontiers of each other's being. It is in conversation that the newness of each participant can come forth and the unconditioned can be revealed in new forms of gesture and language.

The receptive listener frees the speaker to let the unformed emerge into new awarenesses, and the interchange which follows has the possibility of moving both speaker and listener to new heights of being.

Educational activity is activity not only between man and man, however. It also involves activity between the student and other beings in the world. The student encounters other people and natural and man-made phenomena. To these he has the ability to respond. Indeed, education may be conceived to be the influencing of the student's response-ability. The student is introduced to the wealth and beauty of the phenomenal world, and is provided with the encouragement to test out his response-abilities until they call forth the meaning of what it is to be thrown into a world as a human being.

Here, then, are concepts which might possibly be used in an ethical rationality of educational activity: response-ability, conversation, influence, promise, and forgiveness. How can these concepts be used to explore the meanings of classroom activity?

First, the sanctity of response-ability and speech must be recognized. The human being with his finite freedom and his potential participation in the creation of the world, introduces newness and uniqueness into the world, and contributes to the unveiling of the unconditioned by the integrity of his personal, spontaneous responsiveness. His responses to the world in which he finds himself are tokens of his participation in this creative process, and must be accepted as such. Forcing responses into preconceived, conditioned patterns inhibits this participation in the world's creation. Limiting response-ability to existing forms of responsiveness denies others of their possibility of evolving new ways of existing.

Speech may be considered a basic form of man's response-in-the-world. Indeed, Heidegger[10] equates speech with man's reply as he listens to the world. New speech, poetic nonritualistic or non-conditioned speech, is part of this creative unfolding of the world, and demands from the other a response in kind. The expressions of young children may be pure poetry, in that they can reveal to the adult previously unnoticed newness and possibility. The new theories of the scientist are likewise poetic statements which partake of this joy of creation. Unfortunately, the expressive statements of young children are too frequently ignored or pushed into the venerable coin of the realm by tired adult questions or conditioned responses, and science is taught as a body of knowns and sure things rather than as an activity of man which

[10] Martin Heidegger. *Being and Time.* Translated by John MacQuarrie and Edward Robinson. New York: Harper and Row, 1962.

illuminates the unknown *and* man's poetic character. To accept the non-conditioned speech and response of the student is to accept him, and in so doing to accept the emergence of the unformed and to-be-formed in the world.

Next, knowledge and other cultural forms must be seen as vehicles for responsibility, conversation, and promise. The various disciplines—mathematics, biology, physics, history, sociology, visual arts, drama and others—are not only bodies of principles, concepts, generalizations and syntax to be learned. They are patterned forms of response-in-the-world, which carry with them the possibilities of the emergence of novelty and newness. Introducing the child to the language or symbols and methods of geography or chemistry or music or sculpture is not to introduce him to already existing forms of human existence which he must know in order to exist. Rather these disciplines increase his ability to respond to the world, they increase his response-ability in the world and thus aid in the creation and re-creation of the world. Through them he finds new ways to partake of the world, and he becomes more aware of what he can become and what man can become.

Furthermore, the existing disciplines are language systems linking men to each other via a vocabulary, a syntax, a semantic and a way of making new language. The botanist is not simply a man who is interested in plants; he is a man who talks botany with other men. Disciplines define language communities with their own symbolic rules, and knowledge facilitates the conversations which may emerge. Knowledge becomes a way of conversing between educator and student about some phenomenon in the world. The educator, as a more experienced member of the language community, responds to the student's speech critically yet supportively. Knowledge, used in the process of educational influence between educator and student, becomes an instrument of promise.

The educator does try to influence, but with the optimism and faith in knowledge as a vehicle to new response-abilities and to new conversational possibilities. In essence, he says to the student, "Look, with this knowledge I can promise you that you can find new wonders in the world; you can find new people who can interest you; and in so finding you can discover what you are and what you can become. In so doing you can help discover what man is, has been, and can be. With this knowledge I promise you, not enslavement, not a reduction of your power, but fulfillment and possibility and response-ability." The real teacher feels this promise. He knows the tinge of excitement as the student finds new joys, new mysteries, new power, and new awareness that a full present leads to a future. Too often today, promise is replaced by demand, responsibility by expectations, and conversation by telling, asking and answering.

Finally, ethical rationality for thinking about educational activity provides the concept of forgiveness. This comes from the educator's awareness that with the power to influence is the power to be influenced. To avoid hubris, the educator must accept the possibility of error—error as he influences and as he has been influenced. Hence forgiveness becomes necessary as a way of freeing one's self and the other from the errors of the past. Forgiveness unties man from the past that he may be free to contribute to new creation. With the power to forgive and to be forgiven, the educator dares to influence and to be influenced in the present. With the possibility of forgiveness the student dares to express himself, to leap into the unknown, and to respond with the totality of his being. As long as man is finite, promise must be accompanied by the possibility of forgiveness, otherwise only the old, the known, the tried and tested will be evoked. Because the educator dares to influence, he must have the courage to permeate classroom activity with the ever present possibility of forgiveness; for if he does not, his influence carries with it seeds of destruction through omniscience which can be only demonic.

Aesthetic Rationality

When classroom activity is viewed from the point of view of an aesthetic rationality, quite different categories of meaning are derived. As with the ethical, a variety of aesthetic viewpoints is possible, but Paul Valery's[11] view will be used here. The general scheme is that the teacher creates an aesthetic object to which the students respond. Their responses may also be considered aesthetic objects to which the teacher responds as a critic. The intent throughout classroom activity is not a search for preconceived ends but a search for beauty, for integrity and form and the peace which accompanies them, and for truth as life is unveiled through the acting and speaking of the participants.

Valery defines the execution of a work of art as a "transition from disorder to order, from the formless to form, or from impurity to purity, accident to necessity, confusion to clarity."[12] André Maurois expands this by stating that aesthetic "order must dominate an actual disorder . . .

[11] Paul Valery. *Aesthetics.* Translated by Ralph Mannheim. New York: Bollingen Foundation, 1964.

[12] *Ibid.,* p. 158.

the violent universe of the passions, the chaos of color and sound, dominated by a human intelligence. . . . In great music, the torrent of sound seems always on the point of turning into hurricane and chaos, and always the composer, . . . soars over the tempest, reins in the chaos. But it is because the chaos has overwhelmed us that we are moved when it is checked."[13]

The teacher, then, in classroom activity can tame the incipient chaos and dominate it with human intelligence. Classroom activity can seem ready to disintegrate but for the aesthetic order imposed by the teacher. The influence of this ordered disorder upon the student, if it is an object or event of beauty, is to make him mute.[14] But the response is not dead silence, nor a response of admiration, but of "sustained attention."[15] The artist's intent is "to conjure up developments that arouse perpetual desire,"[16] "to exact of his audience an effort of the same quality as his own,"[17] and "to provoke infinite developments in someone."[18]

The students, awed by the teacher's art, can be moved, then, "to the enchanted forest of language . . . with the express purpose of getting lost; far gone in bewilderment, they seek crossroads of meaning, unexpected echoes, strange encounters; they fear neither detours, surprises, nor darkness; but the huntsman who ventures into this forest in hot pursuit of the 'truth,' who sticks to a single continuous path, from which he cannot deviate for a moment on pain of losing the scent or imperiling the progress he has already made, runs the risk of capturing nothing but his shadow."[19] So the student seeks to dominate his newfound chaos by his own intelligence, and as a critic the teacher responds with critical concern but sympathetic intent. Classroom activity unfolds in a rhythmic series of events, which symbolizes the meanings of man's temporal existence.

Here, then, are concepts which could serve in an aesthetic rationality of educational activity: the continual caging of chaos, psychical distance or non-instrumentality, beauty or harmony and form, truth as unveiled meaning, and criticism. How can these concepts be used to explore the meanings of classroom activity? It would be possible to use these notions to discuss the dynamics of teacher-student interaction. Yet more

[13] *Ibid.,* p. 163.
[14] *Ibid.,* p. 58.
[15] *Ibid.,* p. 161.
[16] *Ibid.,* p. 193.
[17] *Ibid.,* p. 161.
[18] *Ibid.,* p. 151.
[19] *Ibid.,* p. 48-49.

fruitful in this day of knowledge and intellectual concerns is to hint at the place of knowledge in educational activity from the point of view of aesthetic rationality.

First, knowledge can be viewed as the ordering of particular bits of chaos. The irrational or unconditioned constantly creeps out of all forms of knowledge. As Jaspers states:

We become aware of the fact that in cognition we have moved in categories which, even in their totality, are like a fine filigree with which we grasp what at the same time we conceal with it . . . pushing ahead restlessly into the ocean of Being, we find ourselves always again and again at the beach of categorically secure, definite, particular knowledge.[20]

In science it creeps out through the continual destruction and construction of existing concepts and theories through the methodologies of science. In social ideologies it creeps out through the onslaught of circumstance. Thus in teaching, educational activity must order, but the unbridled chaos should not be hidden from the student. To do so is to deprive him of the element which calls forth the mute response, the "sustained attention" and the "perpetual desire."

The psychical distance or non-instrumentality of valued educational activity means that the playful involvement with the tools and products of knowledge need not be subjugated to the demands of social or biological necessity. The teacher and the students can be freed from the demands of utilitarianism, and the classroom can become a place where the purity and beauty of knowledge may be enjoyed for itself. The student can be freed to use knowledge to heighten his own significance, to enlarge his own sensitivities to the world, and to realize what he could be. The near infinite possibilities of knowledge and knowing can be hinted at, and the mysteries of the world can be pointed to without the need to reduce them to problems to be solved.

Aesthetically valued, knowledge has more than power; it has beauty. As a man-made form its balance and harmony, its composition, its integrity and wholeness, point to the peaceful possibilities inherent in human existence. The scientist, the engineer, as well as the artist, are creative artists who engage in the creative evolution of new forms and who bring harmony to a discordant world. Participating in the making of his own knowledge, the student can recognize his inherent potential to add to, and conversely to subtract from, the possibility of man-made beauty. Intellectual disciplines as well as aesthetic crafts are vehicles for this continuing creation.

[20] Karl Jaspers. *Truth and Symbol.* Translated by Jean T. Wilde, William Kluback and William Kimmel. New York: Twayne Publishers, 1959. p. 38 and 79.

As an aesthetic form, knowledge in educational activity becomes symbolic of man's meanings and of his discovered truths. Knowledge as an aesthetic form is a token of man's responsiveness to his own feelings and inner life and to his being a part of its world. Scientific forms of knowledge point to man's willingness to listen to and observe the world around him and to be conditioned by the unknown world. Technical forms of knowledge are symbolic of man's power over the world, and of his desire to shape the world into his own image. Knowledge treated as having an existence beyond the individual or separated from man may be symbolic of man's unwillingness to assume responsibility for his own condition. Knowledge being made and remade in educational activity may symbolize that the educator recognizes that his knowledge is but one of the flowers of his life, which blooms and dies, and yet is the seed of new life.

Finally, the act of criticism becomes a part of the aesthetic process. All aesthetic events and forms must be able to withstand the criticism of knowledgeable and responsible critics. The utterances and acts of teacher and student are proper targets of sympathetic but critical concern. Scientific criteria of empirical validity, parsimony, and logical structure are instruments for the criticism of scientific knowledge. Pragmatic considerations can be a form of criticism of social ideologies. Teacher and students, through their conversations, engage in the mutual criticism of each other's orderings, and thus contribute to the continued transcendence of form over chaos.

In conclusion, present curricular language is much too limited to come to grips with the problems, or rather the mysteries, of language and meaning of the classroom. The educator must free himself from his self-confining schemas, in order that he may listen anew to the world pounding against his intellectual barriers. The present methodologies which govern curricular thought must eventually give away.

Identifying and proposing a solution to the twofold problem of describing and valuing educational activity identified in this paper is but one attempt, among many that should be made, to reformulate aspects of curricular language. With it other meanings of classroom activity might be identified. As Conant points out, the significance of scientific theory is not its validity, but its fruitfulness. The scientific value of these roughly sketched ideas will be their fruitfulness. Their technical and political value are of no significance. Their ethical and aesthetic meanings may be pondered.

Curriculum and the Analysis of Language

Philip H. Phenix

PHILOSOPHICAL inquiry in England and America today is largely analytical in method and critical in temper. The modern movement toward critical analysis gained its early impetus from studies in mathematics and logic by such men as Peano and Frege, whose work was taken up and developed into a full-scale system of symbolic logic in the *Principia Mathematica* of A. N. Whitehead and Bertrand Russell. Analysis has also been the keynote of the most productive work in the philosophy of science in the present century. Einstein's relativity theories were a direct consequence of applying rigorous logical thinking to the fundamental processes of physical measurement, and the quantum mechanical theory of matter and energy was built upon scrupulous concern for logical precision.

Though mathematics and physics proved most amenable to precise logical investigation, the methods of critical systematic analysis have not been restricted to these fields. Shortly after 1900 the influential English philosopher, G. E. Moore, began to develop analytical techniques for examining the import of ordinary language in a variety of fields of inquiry. Bertrand Russell also extended his concerns to language usage generally, and in this effort was joined by many other logicians, preeminent among whom were Rudolph Carnap and Ludwig Wittgenstein. Wittgenstein, who at first emphasized the improvement of understanding through the construction of artificial symbolic systems, in his later years became the leading exponent of ordinary language analysis, which now largely preoccupies technical philosophers in England and America.

The analytical outlook differs markedly from two other approaches that have been dominant in the history of philosophy, namely, the speculative and the ideological. Speculative philosophy, which is concerned with building comprehensive systems of thought about the universe, is perhaps represented in its most extreme form in the philosophy of Hegel, although the great cosmological system of Whitehead is hardly less impressive an achievement, and one that is doubly interesting because it was created by one of the founders of modern mathematical logic. I include in the ideological category philosophies that are primarily concerned with promoting a particular method of looking at knowledge as the only admissible one. The four leading contemporary ideological philosophies are Marxism, pragmatism, logical positivism, and existentialism, each of which, despite denials of the charge, does purport to exhibit the one true way to understanding. The two categories—speculative and ideological—are not mutually exclusive. For example, Marxism and pragmatism both have marked speculative components. Both nonanalytic types of philosophy have in common the quality of system, one stressing content or conclusion and the other emphasizing method.

Analytic Philosophy

Analytic philosophy departs from both speculative and ideological philosophy in its concern for the detailed piecemeal study of the varieties of human signification. The analyst avoids any prescription of method or any comprehensive description of reality. He rather limits himself to the careful investigation of some of the many different ways in which people talk about experience. His attitude is open and tentative. He does not attempt to find any single key to the interpretation of the world, but patiently proceeds to make distinctions and to show relationships among the vast array of possible modes of interpretation.

Philosophical analysis is not a new invention or discovery. It is, in fact, the most ancient and venerable of the ways of philosophizing. For the most part it is the way of Socrates, of Aristotle, and of St. Thomas. It is also an important ingredient even in the system-builders and the methodological monists. In the present century, chiefly under the tutelage of the exact sciences and encouraged by their prestige and success, analysis has risen to a dominant position in professional philosophy, complementing and criticizing the efforts of both kinds of systematizers.

Since philosophy of education consists in the philosophical consideration of educational practice, the character of this branch of philosophy depends on one's general philosophic attitude and approach. Until the last ten or fifteen years philosophy of education has been almost exclusively of the speculative and ideological types. The standard approach in courses in this subject was, and to a considerable extent still is, to present the various systems of philosophy, such as idealism and realism, or the various methodological ideologies such as pragmatism, Marxism, existentialism, and logical positivism, so as to exhibit the supposed "educational implications" of each "ism."

It is now becoming increasingly recognized that this approach to educational orientation through philosophic systems is at best of very limited validity and at worst seriously misleading. One difficulty is that educational practices are not related to theoretical philosophies in any pattern of simple deductive inference, as the "isms" approach assumes. Another related problem is that the issues and the categories that are appropriate to the discussion of educational concerns do not coincide with those that are used in setting up the various systems of philosophy. The attempt to fit educational issues into neat systematic packages according to speculative or methodological criteria thus proves to be a questionable exercise in pedantic ingenuity.

Into this situation of sterile academicism, philosophical analysis has brought new hope for the philosophy of education. A fresh start has been made by returning in piecemeal fashion to the patient, critical exploration of educational issues, without any attempt to comprehend everything within a single grand scheme or to comprise all inquiry within a single methodological framework.

Accordingly, in recent years a new analytic movement in educational thought has rapidly emerged to supplement and, I hope, eventually to displace the traditional "isms" type of educational philosophy. Thinkers like Israel Scheffler, Robert Ennis, Kingsley Price, and James McClellan have begun to produce and collect a considerable body of literature dealing with educational ideas from the standpoint of logical analysis. Much of the analysts' attention has been devoted to the careful discussion of the various uses to which such educational terms as "teaching," "learning" and "knowing" are put, with the aim of demonstrating by typical examples that no single definition will suffice, but that a number of different interrelated logical constructions must be distinguished. In view of these distinctions, the analysts show that broad generalizations about the process of education, which are standard for the speculative and ideological types of educational philosophy, have no specifiable meaning, but serve mainly as slogans for the propagation of special pedagogical interests.

From the pursuit of the analysis of educational language, a further consequence ensues that I believe has not been clearly enough noticed even by many who espouse and employ analytic methods. A thoroughgoing treatment of an educational concept such as "learning" shows not only that no satisfactory idea of learning-in-general can be set forth, but that one cannot even do justice to this concept by making a variety of generalized distinctions such as between "learning that," "learning how," and "learning why," that is, between fact, skill, and explanation uses of "learning," even when these types are further analyzed into a number of distinct typical sub-uses.

It is now becoming evident that the significance of educational ideas cannot be assessed apart from a detailed analysis of the specific contexts in which they are employed. What are these specific contexts? The answer to this question depends on the content of the curriculum, which includes the various distinctive types of experiences into which the student is guided. Now the school is not a separate and autonomous institution. It is one institution among others in an interdependent cultural complex. If the school is to serve the needs of real persons in a real society, the curriculum must do justice to the many different types of experience that people actually have. Furthermore, in order to give students the benefit of the accumulated wisdom of civilization, so that they do not have to try to recapitulate the whole history of invention and discovery, the curriculum should consist of opportunities for experience selected so as to make available to the learner the best organized and the most productive insights. In view of the vast amount of knowledge that can be learned and the relatively limited time in which to learn it, careful selection of curricular materials should be made, eliminating not only what is misleading and erroneous, but also everything that is routine, commonplace, uncritical and superficial.

Disciplined Inquiry

As I have argued at length elsewhere, the curricular materials meeting the requirements of a modern school are derived from scholarly and professional disciplines. Disciplined knowledge is that which is produced by communities of expert inquirers whose efforts have proven reliably fruitful in insight and fresh discoveries. The task of the educator, then, is to introduce students to the methods and results of disciplined inquiry, thereby mediating to the nonspecialist the cognitive benefits of the major areas of specialized investigation.

The disciplines are also the basis for distinguishing the sub-types of knowledge into which analytic inquiry ought to be directed. The various disciplines differ by virtue of the different kinds of things investigated and the different conceptual schemes used in the process of investigating. They represent a primary source of conceptual discriminations that mark the path for philosophical analysis to follow. The meaning of "learning" cannot be stated in general or even in certain broad limiting categories. Instead, it ought to be analyzed within the context of each discipline, to show what it signifies under the actual conditions in which knowledge is gained and validated. "Learning" in mathematics is not the same as "learning" in biology, in morals, or in history. Each discipline has its characteristic ways of learning, which should be the object of analytic investigation.

It seems clear that the study of typical concepts and methods in the disciplines is the task to which philosophical analysis may most profitably be directed. Such an approach emphasizes the virtual identity of philosophy and philosophy of education, for the divisions into which philosophic study naturally falls are mainly the disciplines, which also constitute the basis for the curriculum. In this connection it is interesting that a recent series of thirteen introductory studies in the "Foundations of Philosophy," edited by Elizabeth and Monroe Beardsley, includes eight that deal with specific discipline areas, namely, mathematics, language, natural science, social science, art, morals, history, and religion. Two others, logic and theory of knowledge, concern problems which underlie analysis of the specific discipline areas. The study of metaphysics, which is in large part a philosophy of human nature, as well as the study of political philosophy, are also both fundamental to the consideration of educational issues. The one other study, entitled *Philosophy of Education,* is manifestly concerned explicitly with education.

The point of emphasis in all this is that, in order to be fruitful and relevant, both philosophy and education must be related directly to what specialized investigators are doing in the various disciplines. Philosophies of everything-in-general, as propounded by the system-builders and congealed in the "isms" of their followers, no longer represent a sufficient interpretation of human experience. Modern philosophy must be closely linked with what is actually going on in the specific areas of disciplined investigation. Likewise, the curriculum needs to be directly related to the various disciplines of knowledge.

In thus stressing piecemeal analysis and the specialized disciplines, I may appear to be ruling out the integrative element in both philosophy and education. Surely there is a great need in modern culture for unifying ideas and ideals to encourage personal and social coordination. It would be a matter for regret if the growth of specialization should only increase the fragmentation of modern life. Fortunately, there are disciplines that are specifically designed to serve the purposes of integration. Their characteristic concepts and methods are chosen so as to reveal significant relationships. Philosophy itself is integrative, especially in such branches as metaphysics, epistemology, logic, and social philosophy, in which interpretive categories of wide applicability are developed. The disciplines of history, religion, and literature are also synoptic in perspective, as are some of the more concrete empirical sciences, including anthropology, sociology, political science, and geography.

Philosophy goes astray when its integrative function is conceived in the manner of a monolithic system or method, for the result of such restriction is just the opposite of unification, namely, the generation of sectarian philosophical orthodoxies. Furthermore, education organized under the guidance of such philosophies is diverted from its proper connection with the living sources of culture. For example, an existentialist, a Thomist, or an experimentalist philosophy of education, seriously applied, would impoverish teaching and learning by directing attention too narrowly to certain aspects of experience. In contrast, philosophy of education conceived analytically is open to the full range of possibilities for the interpretation of experience. It is not designed to provide a grand alternative to the detailed insights of the many specialized disciplines, as the systematic and ideological philosophies in effect aim to do, but to contribute to the logical interpretation and symbolic elucidation of the knowledge coming from every domain of human experience, including the whole spectrum of organized disciplines.

Logical Analysis of Language
in the Disciplines

I want now to illustrate the sort of contribution that philosophy conducted as the logical analysis of language in the disciplines can make to educational theory and practice. For this purpose I shall cite several introductory studies, each dealing in an analytical fashion with one discipline in the curriculum.

Ordinary Language

The first reference is a collection of analytical essays entitled *Philosophy and Ordinary Language*, edited by Charles E. Caton. Philosophical analysts have given considerable attention to the logical structure of ordinary language. Though often concerned with what seem to be inconsequential trivia, their discussions are of direct relevance to language education. First, analysis encourages due respect for the subtlety and complexity of ordinary language. In an essay in the Caton volume, J. L. Austin, for example, shows that there is no sense to questions about the meaning of a word in general. Individual words ordinarily do not have meaning; sentences do. Hence the meaning of a word must always be determined by reference to its syntactics and semantics, that is, to the kinds of sentences in which its use is appropriate (and inappropriate) and to the sorts of experiences to which it is (and is not) relevant. The analytically guided language teacher will help his students toward a dynamic, functional, and organic approach to language, in which words are not studied in isolation, but always in relation to other words in complex syntactic structures and with reference to specific uses.

In view of this complexity, the logical analyst is a critic of all simple and absolute distinctions. Thus, in another essay, Austin discusses the common distinction between performative utterances, which are actions (e.g., "I welcome you"), and constative utterances (e.g., "I am an American"), which declare something to be the case. The customary distinction is that constative utterances are either true or false, but that such judgments do not apply to performative utterances. Analysis soon discloses that this clear-cut distinction does not hold, since both kinds of utterances are subject to much the same sorts of problems, involving appropriateness to the situation, attitude of the speaker, degree of precision, etc. Thus, truth or falsity is not a simple criterion but "a whole dimension of criticism," which may apply to different sorts of utterances.

Similarly, S. E. Toulmin and K. Baier in their chapter analyze the distinction that C. K. Ogden and I. A. Richards made between descriptive and emotive expressions, and show that no such simple division can be defended, since there are many different ways of classifying the utterances of ordinary discourse, and these classifications cut across one another in complex fashion. The authors further illustrate a number of the different kinds of distinctions that can be made in analyzing linguistic expressions.

The language analyst is an enemy of Procrustean beds and of pedantic abstractions. He warns teachers and students against the temptation to oversimplify language study by a tidy set of labels and a few facile generalizations. In urging the student of language to attend more carefully to the ways speech is actually used, in all its variety and subtlety, he helps him to understand the depth, range and power of human symbolization.

Philosophical analysis also directly demonstrates how language instruction may be carried out. In fact, analysis is itself an example of education in linguistic usage. Two features of this teaching are especially noteworthy. The first is the pervasive use of concrete examples. The analyst makes his case by citing cases. He shows what he means by citing characteristic illustrations, and he tests the limitations of his generalizations by means of boundary examples where the generalizations cease to hold. By using typical cases, he fosters the habit of looking at expressions in terms of the roles they perform in actual communication, rather than in terms of some *a priori* static rules of grammar or dictionary meaning.

A second pedagogical insight of analysis is contained in the analogy of language with games, as first explained by Wittgenstein. The roles played by various kinds of expressions are in important respects like the roles associated with the various pieces in a game like chess. Each piece is capable of certain characteristic moves that are defined by the rules of the game. Similarly, the uses appropriate to various linguistic expressions are governed by the conventional rules of the language game. This concept of verbal play not only helps the student to grasp the characteristic features of language as a discipline and thus to discriminate between essential and nonessential features; it is also likely to appeal more to his imagination and to arouse more interest than the traditional approach to language as a body of vocabulary and correct grammatical forms to be memorized.

Mathematics

As in the case of language, mathematics is comprised of symbolic systems defined by certain arbitrary rules. This insight is fundamental in the treatment of mathematics by the analytic philosophers. In fact, as I indicated earlier, modern philosophical analysis developed in part out of mathematical logic. The theory of sets, which has played such a central role in some of the new mathematics curricula, is substantially identical with the logic of classes that underlay the analytical studies of

Frege and Russell. The concept of sets, or classes, is basic from an analytic standpoint because it enables one to identify with precision a collection of entities all of which are related by some common rule. It provides a means of distinguishing entities that belong to a specifiable collection from those that do not. Thus the idea of sets, or classes, is implicit in the making of precise distinctions. This ability is important for all rigorous thinking, in mathematics as well as in other domains of thought. The modern teaching of mathematics is actually instruction in logical analysis. Its objective is the development of skill in the definition and transformation of systems of symbols according to specified arbitrary rules.

An unusually clear and illuminating treatment of mathematics by an analytic philosopher may be found in Friedrich Waismann's *Introduction to Mathematical Thinking,* which draws heavily on the classic work of the mathematician Felix Klein (in his *Elementary Mathematics from a Higher Standpoint*) as well as the thought of the philosopher Wittgenstein. Waismann's book is largely devoted to the analysis of the elemental concept of number. He shows that it is not possible to assign any clear meaning to the idea of number in general, but only with respect to specified calculation rules. Thus, the cardinal numbers comprise one self-contained consistent system, the integers (positive and negative) a second distinct system, the rational numbers a third, the real numbers a fourth, and the imaginary numbers a fifth. Each number system has its own characteristic rules of operation that distinguish it from all the other systems.

Waismann's analysis shows that the common sense intuitive approach to the various kinds of numbers leads to basic confusions and to a complete misconception of mathematical ways of thinking. Under the intuitive approach, all numbers belong to a single large class of quantitative entities. Cardinal numbers are identified with positive integers, negative integers are regarded simply as backward extensions of cardinal numbers, and rational numbers are taken as ratios of integers. Real numbers and imaginary numbers are further mysterious extensions that enable one to solve equations that are not soluble by the simpler kinds of numbers.

This rule-of-thumb arithmetical expediency wholly obscures the most essential feature of mathematical thought, namely, the postulational method. From the very earliest years the student of mathematics should be instructed in the playful art of constructing freely chosen symbol systems, the elements of which are combined by specified rules. The crucial idea is that all mathematical reasoning must take place *within a given system*. One may not validly carry out a mathematical argument that straddles two or more postulational systems. Even in the elementary matter of numbers the distinction between systems must be observed. Each kind of number belongs to its own postulational system. If the student understands this principle, he will be in possession of the sovereign means of attaining clarity throughout the study of mathematics, at every level. When the method of system-thinking is grasped, the student may profitably complement it by the analysis of formal similarities between systems. For example, the calculating rules for the various types of numbers are alike in important respects. That is why it is so easy to make the mistake of regarding them as all members of one class.

The essence of mathematical thinking is to understand both the idea of system identity and integrity and the idea of isomorphic relations that preserve the calculating rules from system to system. One of the main uses of the philosophical analysis of mathematical language is to guide the teaching and study of mathematics in the light of these two fundamental ideas.

Physical Science

In an earlier paragraph I have already mentioned the close connection between the rise of contemporary philosophical analysis and the development of modern physics. It is not surprising, therefore, that the philosophy of physical science today is largely informed by the methods and spirit of analysis. An example of this approach may be found in Stephen Toulmin's *Philosophy of Science: An Introduction*. The analytic study of the methods and concepts of physics is of far-reaching significance for science education; it revolutionizes one's whole outlook on the subject. Any general idea of scientific method, which students are supposed to learn in science courses, is shown to be untenable. Not only is there no general method of thinking; there is not even a general rule for thinking in science. Scientific discovery and validation are many-faceted processes that can only be understood by detailed piecemeal critical investigation.

As an illustration, Toulmin analyzes the principle of geometrical optics that light travels in straight lines. He shows that this is not a fact that can be directly observed, nor is it a straightforward generalization based on a number of particular observations. Rather, it is a way of thinking and talking about light that proves to be useful in drawing inferences. It is a mode of representing light that enables one to give a satisfactory account of certain optical phenomena.

It is easy to see how valuable such an insight can be to the physics teacher. It suggests at least two questions that will lead the student right to the heart of physical inquiry. The first is: "What other ways of representing light can be devised, and how well would they do the job of accounting for what is observed?" By asking this question the student is introduced to the meaning of scientific imagination and model construction which are basic to all productive scientific investigation.

The second question that grows out of analyzing the logic of this physical principle is: "What is the experimental context within which the model of rectilinear propagation applies?" It evidently works well for the phenomenon of shadow casting, but not for refraction, diffraction, scattering, and photoelectric effects, which require different methods of representation, including wave and particle models. In this fashion the student learns to regard physical principles not as statements of fact that are either true or false, but as techniques of inference that have specified contexts of application. The symbolisms of physics, like those of ordinary language and of mathematics, have certain functions to perform. It is the goal of analysis to delineate those functions and their scope of application, and thus to chart the various paths along which productive inquiry may proceed.

The centrality of creative imagination is also manifest in analyzing the logic of laws in physics. A law is not simply an inductive generalization based on observations. It is the form of a regularity that has to be surmised before any meaningful observations can be made. Toulmin points out the decisive difference in this respect between the procedure of the physicist and that of the naturalist. The latter starts with observation. He studies the world of things as they present themselves in nature, and devises a language of classification to represent the forms he finds. The physicist, on the other hand, begins with an idea, which is often expressed in a mathematical formula, concerning certain theoretical relationships that can be tested by observation, and only then does he construct experiments that will determine whether, to what degree, and under what conditions these relationships hold.

One of the most illuminating results of the logical analysis of physics is the analogy that Toulmin draws between physical theories and maps. Students are generally familiar with various kinds of maps, and they understand that the type of map used depends on the use one intends to make of it. For example, a map for purposes of aerial navigation is quite different from one used for making an automobile trip, and both differ from a map used in oil prospecting. It is important to know that theories in science are in many respects like maps. They guide the experimenter in successful experimental journeys. They are ways of looking at the world that are productive of results in investigation. Like maps, they are abstract ideal constructions designed to serve in specific types of experimental situations. The student who grasps the cartographic logic of scientific theory will have taken a major step toward understanding the methods of exact science.

Aesthetics

One might be tempted to think that while logical analysis may be useful in the sciences and mathematics and in the technical investigation of ordinary language, it would not apply to the study of the humanistic disciplines. This is not the case. In fact, it can be argued that the analytical approach is peculiarly salutary in the humanities, in order to rescue them from irrationality, confusion and sentimentality, which the scientific disciplines are explicitly designed to minimize.

For example, Virgil C. Aldrich, in his book called *Philosophy of Art*, applies analytic methods to aesthetic problems. He shows that our understanding of both science and art has long been distorted by a misleading subject-object dualism in the theory of perception. According to the standard account, science yields knowledge of objective facts and art is concerned only with subjective feelings. The cultural and educational consequences of this dualism are disastrous. Science is regarded as the only valid source of truth, and art is relegated to the domain of individual private emotions. As in so many other problems, logical analysis upsets this simplistic dichotomy. According to Aldrich, there are different ways of looking at things, each serving a different purpose. "Observation" is one mode of perception, yielding knowledge of qualities. Aesthetic "prehension" is another equally valid mode of perception, in which other characteristics of material things are realized in experience. These other characteristics are not the measured properties of scientific description, but objective impressions or "aspects" that "animate" the objects perceived. Both physical and aesthetic perception presuppose minds entering into relation with material objects. Both are inescapably at the same time subjective *and* objective. Yet material things are perceived according to different and equally valid categories in the two cases, namely, those of physical space and of aesthetic space, respectively.

Once the status of aesthetic experience has thus been established, a second task of analysis is to delineate the various factors that enter into a work of art, including materials, medium, content, subject matter, and form. These factors, each of which needs to be further analyzed in detail, comprise a framework into which the intelligent consideration of works of art can be set, both for those who are learning to make them and for those who seek to appreciate them. These analytic concepts provide a symbolic system in terms of which the creation and enjoyment of art objects can fruitfully proceed. Thus, they constitute basic foci of emphasis for the teaching of the arts. They are primary categories for aesthetic instruction and topics for the agenda of art education.

Yet the analytic thinker in aesthetics is not content with making distinctions about aesthetic experience in general or even about the part of it that is concerned with works of art. He goes on to distinguish the specific meanings of the various artistic factors in the several arts, stressing the characteristic features of each art that follow from utilizing its particular materials.

A third task of analysis in the arts is to provide a basis for critical evaluation. If aesthetic experience is not merely inchoate subjective emotion, then it must be possible to make defensible judgments about the meaning and worth of works of art. Such judgments presuppose that objects of art have logical structures to which standards of excellence can be applied. The person educated in aesthetic matters should be able to give good reasons for prizing a particular work of art. It is not enough merely to state preferences. The special contribution of analytic philosophy to the field of criticism has been twofold: First, it has helped to provide an array of relatively clear concepts for speaking about aesthetic objects. Second, it has turned critics away from large scale, general categories of judgment, whether psychological, metaphysical, or theological, and focused attention on the values inherent in individual works of art. Such individual intersubjective norms are the only kind that are consonant with the essential logic of aesthetic meaning. The analytic insistence on discovering the reasons for preferring a work of art within the work itself is one of the controlling principles of aesthetic education.

Ethics

Moral or ethical education presents some of the same problems as aesthetic instruction, since both are concerned with action (making or doing) and with judgments of value. A good example of introductory ethical analysis may be found in R. M. Hare's book, *The Language of Morals*. Just as Aldrich had to clear away the prejudice that empirical observation is the only kind of objective perception, so also must Hare argue a basic preliminary point in ethics that statements of fact are not the only kind of sentences to which we can give good reasons for assent. Hare establishes the point by an analysis of prescriptive language generally, of which the language of morals is a part.

The clearest case of prescription is the imperative, which discussion shows to be a close logical kinsman to the value judgment. The irreducible logical difference between statements and commands is that the former are indications of *believing* something, while the latter are attempts to induce action. Moreover, because of this logical difference, no amount of factual information can ever by itself add up to an imperative conclusion. Every imperative conclusion must be justified in part by reference to some imperative premise.

This analytic insight about the irreducibility of prescriptives to indicatives is of fundamental importance for moral instruction. It suggests that responsible moral persons can never be nurtured by being taught only facts. No accumulation of information can tell anyone what he ought to do. The ideal of the teacher as one who remains uncommitted and adheres to objective facts without involving himself in judgments of value or affirmations of obligation thus proves to be far from ideal. Sound moral judgment requires not only knowledge of the facts but a substantial stock of well-tested moral principles (prescriptions) for the guidance of conduct.

Important as principles are, they are not sufficient for moral growth. The other essential element is practice in making deliberate choices. The centrality of choice making comes out with particular force in Hare's analysis of the meaning of the term "good." He argues that "good" is not an indefinable quality, like "yellow," as G. E. Moore and other intuitionists held, but that "good" is to be defined with reference to the act of choosing. One regards a thing as the "best" among several alternatives if it is the one he would choose to fulfill the function for which it is intended. That is to say, the choice is guided by some standard of preference. This holds both for nonmoral choices, where the standards are those of functional efficiency, and for moral choices, where nonfunctional standards of virtue apply. In every case, the essence of evaluative judgments is rational preferences manifest in making choices.

The teacher who understands the logic of morality will insure, first, that his students are well supplied with moral principles, representing the accumulated practical wisdom of the past; second, that they learn how to use their factual knowledge to assess the effects that follow from taking particular actions and from adhering to certain principles of action; third, that they gain skill in reflecting about the whole way of life with which particular actions and principles of action cohere; and finally, that they have ample opportunity actively to choose what they will do in concrete cases, to reconstruct the array of principles upon which they rely for direction, and to elect the total pattern of life with which they intend to become identified.

Analytical ethical theory clearly does not provide the teacher with a catalog of virtues to be taught, any more than aesthetic analysis reveals the content of the beautiful, or analytic philosophy of science yields knowledge of the laws of nature. In each discipline the office of analysis is to suggest the terms in which inquiry can fruitfully proceed and to keep attention focused on matters that are relevant to the characteristic purposes of the study being pursued. The special contribution of ethical analysis, on the one hand, is to save moral judgments from irrationality and subjectivism, and on the other, to rescue them from objectification either through intuitionist introspection or naturalistic reduction, by pointing to the centrality of principled choice, informed by pertinent factual knowledge.

Religion

Finally, let us look briefly at the pedagogical importance of the philosophical analysis of the language of religion. Of all the disciplines, one might suppose religious studies to be the most unpromising for analytic treatment, concerned as they are with matters that transcend the world of finite affairs. The positivistic ideologists did (and still do) dismiss religious utterances as meaningless. In recent years, however, this dogmatism has somewhat waned, and a number of respectable analytic philosophers have begun to work in the philosophy of religion. In doing so, they are reestablishing an ancient tradition, for many of the classical theological controversies, particularly in Christendom, have been conducted from the standpoint of the analysis of symbol systems.

A good example of an elementary approach to the analytic philosophy of religion may be found in Ian T. Ramsey's book, *Religious Language: An Empirical Placing of Theological Phrases*. Ramsey begins by describing the kinds of situations in which the use of religious language is appropriate. These are principally of two kinds, namely, those of discernment and those of commitment. Discernment situations are ones in which a fresh and unexpected disclosure occurs, yielding a new insight into the depths of meaning in experience. Commitment situations are ones in which a person is grasped by a sense of the intrinsic worth of something to which he is willing to dedicate himself. Both types of situations are most fully exemplified in the experience of worship, in which discernment takes the form of joyous wonder at the revelation of love manifest in the gift of existence, and in which commitment consists in reverent devotion to the source of all being.

Of course, not all discernment and commitment situations are religious. They become religious whenever ordinary insight and devotion become occasions for worship, that is, for acknowledging the infinite mystery of being and the unconditional quality of one's dedication to its ground. However, ordinary situations do provide models for the formulation of theological ideas. For example, the idea of God as First Cause is based on the model of causation drawn from the ordinary discernment of connections between events. The qualifier "First" indicates that the model of dependence or derivation applies in a superordinary sense, that is, within a worship situation. The term "First" in this expression does not indicate the initial member of a finite series of causes, but the mysterious depth of causality in which all causation is grounded. Similarly, the concept of "good" is a model drawn from ordinary value experience. When it is accompanied by the qualifier "infinitely" to signify one of the divine attributes, it does not connote the end term in a finite ordered sequence of increasing values. It is used rather for expressing complete devotion in a worship situation.

Ramsey characterizes these qualified models as "logically odd." That is to say, their logic is not what their grammatical form would suggest. The logic of the term "First Cause" is not that of members in ordinary causal chains, nor is the logic of the term "infinitely good" that of members in ordinary hierarchies of value. The leap from ordinary to theological import is somewhat analogous to the mathematical process of passing to the limit of an infinite series. Though the idea of a limit is significant, it is never definable by any finite series of steps, but only by the process of successive approximation. Thus mathematical limits have a logic different from that of terms in the series. So also is theological language about the infinite different from but functionally related to the language of ordinary events.

The logical analysis of religious language provides a major clue to the place of religion in the curriculum. It suggests that traditional catechizing is likely to contribute very little to religious understanding. Instead, it appears that every phase of the curriculum offers models of insight and devotion which may eventuate in worship. All studies when pursued in sufficient depth and with enough concern lead into the divine presence. From this standpoint, education is secularized insofar as it remains within the safe limits of finitude, and, on the other hand, any education that encourages students to venture into the ultimate mysteries of being and value is in fact religious and requires appropriate language to express its concerns.

In conclusion, the foregoing examples of analytical treatment in a number of disciplines only suggest in a cursory way the nature of the contribution that language analysis can make to the problems of education. Other disciplines, including biology, psychology, history, and the various social sciences, have also been made the subject of philosophical analysis and might have been cited by way of further illustration. The purpose here is merely to indicate something of the mood and method of analysis and to show the kind of insights that curriculum theorists and practitioners may expect from it.

My main effort has been to sketch the lines along which it seems to me contemporary philosophy of education may most profitably develop. The older speculative systems and the ideological "isms" in my opinion are more likely to distort and mislead than to aid in understanding education. Even some contemporary philosophical analysts of educational concepts fall into the old ways by attempting to explicate the language of education too generally, without regard to the complexities of context. I have argued that the realities of civilized endeavor require consideration of the various organized disciplines as the ways in which inquiry has actually proven successful. Each discipline offers a particular family of concepts and methods that may fruitfully be explored analytically. Furthermore, logical analysis can reveal the similarities and differences between the patterns of inquiry and cognition in the various disciplines. In this way insights may be obtained into the structure of the various disciplines that constitute the basis of civilization and into the interrelationships among the disciplines comprising the curriculum as a whole.

A philosophy of education based upon the logical analysis of the language of the various disciplines is not just another system. It is an always tentative and unfinished array of insights into the many different ways in which the world and human experience may productively be understood. Each discipline provides a set of valuable characteristic perspectives that have a logical structure distinct from those of other disciplines, but bearing certain formal relationships to them. It is the function of the philosopher of education to make clear the logic of the major disciplined perspectives that the curriculum aims to foster, thereby providing a critical and comparative grasp of the organized resources for human understanding.

Illustrative Readings

Language: Charles E. Caton, editor. *Philosophy and Ordinary Language.* Urbana, Illinois: University of Illinois Press, 1963.

Mathematics: Friedrich Waismann. *Introduction to Mathematical Thinking.* New York: Harper Torchbooks, 1959.

Physics: Stephen Toulmin. *The Philosophy of Science, An Introduction.* New York: Harper Torchbooks, 1960.

Art: Virgil C. Aldrich. *Philosophy of Art.* Englewood Cliffs, New Jersey: Prentice-Hall, Inc., 1963.

Ethics: R. M. Hare. *The Language of Morals.* New York: Oxford University Press, 1964.

Religion: Ian T. Ramsey. *Religious Language, An Empirical Placing of Theological Phrases.* New York: The Macmillan Company, 1963.

The Discovery of Felt Meaning

Eugene T. Gendlin

LET me begin with the question: What is thinking? What is "a thought" or "a chain of thought"? In this question I am not asking for a definition or an answer in logic. Instead I want to invite you to pay attention directly to your own thinking. What do you have there? What goes on that you call "thinking"?

For example, just now, you are thinking this question, "what is thinking?" Let us see what this is. First of all there are the words: *What is thinking?* But is that all there is to thinking? Just the resounding of the sounds, the reverberation of the verbal symbols? In addition to sounds you have a feeling of questioning, of expectancy, a sense that you know what these sounds mean—and are asking for and about. You do not have a chance at the moment to elaborate this felt sense of the question. But if you were going to think through more exactly what these words mean, then you would attend to this sense of them, which you have. If you heard some words in a language which you do not know, you would still have the sounds, perhaps you could repeat them to yourself, but you would lack the other part of thinking, the felt sense.

Thus, thinking is not only sounds but also felt sense. Really we should call it a *flow* of felt sens*ing*, not individual bits. Such sensing may seem as if it were only *one* unit, *the* meaning of a given set of words, *the* sense of this question, but when explicated in words, it turns out to be many, *many* things. For example, if you were now to stop reading and instead continue with words of your own, you might now say quite a lot about this question I asked. But if you do not actually work it out in words, you have only this one felt sense of "oh yes"—you know what the question means. Such felt sensing always contains *implicitly*, in one feeling, a great many different facets we *could* explicitly verbalize.

45

Anything we say or think always involves many facets; for instance, the larger point someone is getting at, the whole context of the situation, perhaps also a puzzlement, a sense of something unclear, perhaps conflicting or unresolved, a sense of direction as well as always many other aspects.

A feeling is never just an affective tone, an emotional quality. It is never just "in us." It is always *at,* or *about,* or *for,* or *in* a context of perceptions and events. For example, one never feels anger, as a thing-within, an affective state, inside like undigested food is inside the stomach. Rather, one always feels anger-at something or someone. If we explicate any feeling, it always turns out to *be* a long chain of the following sort: I am angry at Mr. A's doing so and so, which I need to do because if I cannot, I will have to do certain things instead, but I know I will fail when I try them because I am so and so in such situations, which I know I ought to change but cannot, . . . and on and on.

A Living Texture

The first words we use to spell out a felt sense may not seem very promising, e.g., "this feels vague" or "I do not know what you are getting at." Yet, if we explicate the felt sense further, we never find that it is "just" vagueness or confusion. It is always of the sort: what you said seems vague *because* I know you do not mean it to imply "X" (since before you said "Y") but if you do not mean "X" and still it is supposed to apply to that other stuff, then what *do* you mean?" If we really pursue such a felt sense of thinking we produce these long chains of perceptions of the situation, of the conversation, the subject matter. This is also why thinking works, why our felt sense leads to words about the situation we are in. The human being, in fact, any animal, is a highly complex organism. An organism is an ongoing moving system interacting with the environment in which it lives, breathes, digests food and gives off wastes, and against the ground on which it steps and puts pressure. In this environment the animal feels very finely many slight shifts and happenings, as these are significant in the body's life processes of locomotion, digestion, reproduction, respiration, etc. Thus anything "has meaning" in the sense that it affects a living system . . . and affects it therefore always in complexly organized respects. Because the body is a completely organized interaction, therefore, anything that impinges on it has a complex meaning.

In itself, what happens may only be a falling pebble, but when it hits the skin of an animal it may create an impact in the animal which is not only a powerful feeling, but highly organized meanings ... that is to say, the pebble may stir the animal to complex reactions, of intense listening, of utterly still run-ready tensed muscles, of complex felt knowledge of the possible nearness of some foe, of hiding places, of its young to be protected, of pathways to run, of scents to seek, of the direction of wind and oncoming weather, and much more. All this is what I call "implicit" in that first felt impact which the falling pebble stirred.

Feeling is always a living texture of environmental interaction. Therefore the flow of felt sense which—along with verbal sound-images —is our thinking, this flow of felt sense implicitly contains the complex world we live in, the environment, our perceptions, the context of all that has been done and said till now, what is being gotten at, the purpose, the definitions, and a *very* great deal more. And therefore, thinking can be about something, we can arrive at possible truths with it, even though it seems to be only sound echoes and felt sense.

Therefore feeling is capable of being explicated into such complex chains of meanings.

Of course, there is not only felt sense but also logic. In its precise definition, any word, concept or sentence has precise *logical* implications. Any concept is a particular pattern and just certain things will follow. Other implications will not follow, will not be logically consistent with it, will contradict or disorganize the concept if forced onto it. Our logical precision comes from the logical structure, the pattern, the construct character of a concept. We need construct precision, otherwise we could not make sense with language. However, as I have shown, when a human being *thinks* a concept, we have more going on than just the given construct and the implications consistent with it.

The Nature of Concepts

What really is a concept? A concept is both logical and felt. It is a logical construct but since it is also a thought, it has a "soft underbelly," it is made of felt sensing. We "know what it means" or "what we mean by using it" ... we know what we mean with it in a felt sensing way. We mean with the concept to make a certain point, to take exception to an aspect of what has been said, to point out certain things which are important because ... and so on (again the chain of many many implicit facets, as with any felt sense, so with felt sense of a concept-in-use).

When we think (for example about a problem), we use some precise verbalized constructs. We may say these over and over to ourselves: Thereby we review the "givens" of the problem. As we do so, we get the sense of the problem. These givens do not go together. Given this purpose and that fact and that other condition, it will not work out. It is a problem. To solve it, something will have to "give." We will not get the new facet that solves the problem out of the given concepts directly. If we could, it would not be a problem, just an oversight.

To think, we cannot repeat over and over the sentences that say what is given. As long as we keep saying these sentences over and over to ourselves we are not thinking. We have to "know" them well enough to have them in a felt sense, so we can skip the reviewing in words, and just say: "Let us see now, there is this, and this, and that, and we want... yes, that... so..." and then we "mull," that is to say, we depend for new ideas on the felt sense directly. We may say "Oh... just a second, I've got something..." There is a felt sense of "give"[1] (referent movement[1]) but as yet no words. As we explicate in words the new aspect of felt sensing, we may find that we have a step toward a possible solution. Or, as we explicate in words we may find it disappointing or erroneous. Thinking and problem solving always occur as felt sensing and not with only the given verbal conceptual constructs.

We break out of the conceptual boxes to think. After we take a "mulling" felt sensing step, *then* we explicate by modifying the constructs, we make the new step fit in with what really counts about the constructs we had, we make it logically consistent, but we do this by modifying our constructs, by making distinctions, by noting now that we did not really have to mean this or that seeming implication of what we had before. We reformulate the construct so it does not mean that, or we add something. We arrive at something logically consistent and we can fill in the steps we took in a logically consistent way... but only afterwards can we do this. Before we have had the movement of felt sense we only know that something has to be altered, but we cannot know what. The conceptual boxes we had (in the way in which we had them) constituted the problem. The problem can be worked on only by the process of felt sense. How might we make a method of felt sensing? Today we are in a very advanced position to do just that: to use and teach the use of felt meanings *systematically*.

[1] Eugene T. Gendlin. "A Theory of Personality Change." Chapter in: *Personality Change*. Philip Worchel and Donn Byrne, editors. Symposium on Personality Change, University of Texas. New York: John Wiley & Sons, Inc., 1964.

Using the Process of Felt Sensing in Teaching

What we have been saying will remind the reader of the current widespread work on "creativity." Creativity is usually defined as a capacity to get free of given conceptual boxes, given ways of looking at something, given constructs. Not much has yet been said about *what else* there is, other than these constructs which one should hold "loosely" to be creative. Creativity has thus been defined rather negatively: "Don't hold too tightly to your constructs and ways of seeing something." Yet, of course, that is not a helpful instruction, it is not a method you can use, it does not say how and where to look for something new and different, other than the conceptual constructs or perceptions you do have.

Holding tightly or holding ever so loosely—we must say more than that; we must say just where to look and what to do in addition to the constructs we hold loosely. Where to look: at our directly felt sense (which we always have along with words). What to do: pay direct attention to that felt sense and carry it forward, explicate it, put words to it and freshly phrase it, allowing thereby a move in thought along lines that are not just those implied by the logical structure of the constructs we have. Let us make this more specific:

At any point in any discussion we can say to the person speaking: "I don't get what you're driving at. Tell me some other way." The person who has been speaking can always put what he has said another way. Why? Because what he has said was not just the words (he will now use *different* words). He also had a directly felt sense of what he was getting at, trying to say. When we do not grasp this from his words, what does he do? He goes back to his felt sense of what he is trying to say. He pays attention to this directly. He says "Aaaa . . . let me see now, what I really meant was, . . ." and thereby he phrases it freshly. He gets the fresh phrasing not from the constructs and words of what he said, but directly from his felt sense of what it was.

We are all familiar with this when we teach a class. A teacher prepares students in this process, and we can become quite systematic about it. A student says something, often in the form of a question. We answer it, perhaps we are glad that the question brought up something we meant to discuss and so we do. Then we glance at the student who asked the question and he looks . . . well, let us say, rather glum. We know thereby that his effort to get something clarified was unsuccessful. Yet we answered his question—and, let us assume we did a good clear job. Now we say: "I guess that wasn't what you were after!"

He says, no, or perhaps he says, "Oh, that's OK." We say: "But, you were after *something* in asking that... tell us what it was." He says: "Oh, nothing." Yet we know it was something.

In asking that question (any given question) one might be intending *many* different things. People often think something but when they speak they ask a question instead. For example, right now the reader might be thinking: "What he is saying doesn't fit such and such which happens to me when I... etc." If you were now to speak, you might put it in the form of a question: "Have you ever run into a situation where you encounter such and such when you...?" I would then answer, telling about *my* experiences or viewpoints which are probably irrelevant to what happens to you, which puzzles you and which you could tell about.

We tend to begin speaking quite some miles away from what we really mean. If we might like to bring up something, we first test the water, we politely see if we can tease the conversation in the general direction of what we might like to bring up, we ask or comment in a way that is peripheral to what we are really interested in saying. In effect, we ask to be invited to say more, and if that does not succeed, we are perfectly—or almost perfectly—happy, never to say at all what we really meant. It is, therefore, almost always necessary to *invite* people to say more—especially to say *why* they asked or commented as they did, what they were getting at, or just to say *more* about whatever they briefly said or asked.

This applies even when the individual knows exactly what he would like to say. It applies very much more importantly when he does not know exactly, sharply and clearly what he might wish to say or why he thought it interesting to ask, or why specifically something puzzled or struck him. He may have a felt sense but not a worked out verbalized explicit knowledge.

In that case, if as teachers we wish to invite the person further to explicate what he senses or means, we may have to insist. We say, "What were you getting at?" He says: "Oh, nothing." We say: "No, I know you were after something, there when you said so and so, but I just didn't quite get it." He says, "Oh, no, it was nothing it all." Perhaps we give up then and say, "Oh, all right," but we know there was something. Perhaps he finally says, "Well, ah, I guess I'm confused but, ah, well, let me see, ah, well when I try to apply such and so which you mentioned, I get this and this and it doesn't fit in with what you said before." At this point the student *makes sense.*

Perhaps now we can easily show him what he omitted, or perhaps his question is so good that we can't answer it at all, or we can show at what point he diverged from our train of thought. Perhaps his train of thought is also valid, or perhaps it is erroneous. Even if it involves several errors, *it makes sense*, that is to say, we can now see how, given this error and that omission, one *could* see the matter as he does and could wonder about what he wonders about.

It is a basic principle not enough recognized, that feelings always make sense. This does not mean that they are logically or factually correct. On the contrary, to discover the error involved (if an error is involved) is precisely a recognition that—given the error—the erroneous result *does* make sense. But, this requires attention to, and explication of his felt sense.

In fact, very many people have not discovered felt meaning at all. They do not feel that it is worth while or possible to pay such attention to their—always at first vague—felt sensing. They read a book or think some propositions, but they override their fuzzy, slightly disturbing feelings. They never look to see what this "felt something" might be, nor would they expect it ever to become anything more than just a fuzzy feeling. And yet, precisely in that at first fuzzy feeling lies *the individual's reaction to what he reads and says and hears*. We call it his "reaction" only while it still is only a feeling. As he explicates it, it becomes a "good question" or an "original idea" or a "clever insight" or a specific "error." Perhaps the only difference between highly creative original people and those who consider themselves uncreative is whether or not they give this sort of gentle attention and explication to their felt sensing reactions, as they read and think.

It involves a certain attitude of self-worth to give one's felt sensing this kind of patience and attention. At first it is *only* fuzzy. Then, at a second step (moments later) one gets a first formulation, still not usually an attractive one: For example: "This doesn't make sense to me because of that . . ." or "I'm upset when he says such and so because it makes me think of X which I don't like because . . ." But if one bears with this (at first poorly sounding) thought and further explicates one's felt sense of its import or point, one soon comes upon a fully sense-making formulation. One may then be startled by one's capacity for great original thoughts.

A class is quite exciting when the teacher often does this kind of inviting and insisting which leads to the students' discovery of their capacities for original thought.

Moreover—if you have not always done this, you will find it quite exciting: as you read something, you stop reading sometime, and pay attention to the—at first fuzzy feeling you have of the whole thing, to see then, moments later, the budding significance of your thought, as you freshly phrase and explicate the felt sense of what you read, or say, or the words you at first think. But do not look among the abstract sentences for original ideas to come, full blown. The source of further thinking is in that—at first fuzzy—felt sense. Original ideas have their source there where you also feel it when you are hungry or tense. They do not arise full blown and explicit; you must explicate that felt sense.

So far, I have been writing as a teacher. I have been trying to make systematic where to look for, and what to do with—the process which makes for creative thought (and which is, at any rate, an essential aspect of all thought). *Where to look:* there, where we feel hunger, discomfort or relief, for there also we feel directly the sense we make, the point we are after, the thought we have with our words, and the thing we are about to say. *What to do with it:* to pay direct attention to it as felt or sensed, and to allow words to come—words which at first admittedly will be rough and poor—but which freshly phrase and explicate further and further the sense we *implicitly* made. One can do this at any point of any discussion, with any concept or proposition, and one thereby makes transitions and evolves chains of thought which are not limited within one's original words or constructs.

Felt Sensing

Let me now speak as a psychotherapist. This process of *focusing* (Gendlin, 1964[2]) on directly felt ongoing experiencing, *felt meaning* or *felt sense* is also what the patient does in any effective psychotherapy. No matter how the various schools of psychotherapy differ among themselves, whatever constructs they employ, they all agree that real change and resolution of personality trouble comes only through a feeling process, only through the individual's attention to, and *carrying forward* of, his feelings. One's concrete bodily sensed meanings implicitly contain one's whole life context and perceptions. Resolution of personality problems is possible only through concrete movements of felt sensing. Without this, concepts may be as accurate as you please, they may constitute a knowing how it is and how it should be, but they change nothing.

A patient who uses his concepts and words in a "dissociated" way, apart from explicating his felt meanings directly, is said to "intellectualize" or "rationalize." It is well known that intellectualizing does not help. Concepts, no matter how accurate and true, are only general constructs. They tap only a very little of the finely grained com-

[2] Gendlin, *ibid.*

plex organic texture which we are and concretely feel in a bodily way. The patient in psychotherapy changes only if he works with and through that whole, concretely felt texture, itself. Then he moves from step to step through this whole texture. If, on the other hand, he employs concepts *only*, then he is limited. He remains within the implications of the constructs he employs. He can think only just what follows from just those ways of construing which he already has. And so he does not change. He misses, instead of using, that whole complex organic life process within which lie all the many potential meanings of his living and his trouble.

This way of using felt meanings is not a matter of emotional health. I know people who do not use their felt meanings. They see themselves as not very creative, or at least, as not very good thinkers, but many of them are as well adjusted as anybody. This process of focusing on felt meanings is a discovery anyone can make. It is a skill anyone can learn. Research shows that this skill is not the same thing as emotional health.

Therefore, Carl Rogers and I at one time thought that the successful client would begin psychotherapy with little use of felt meaning and then move toward more and more use of his feelings. Research proved us wrong: we found that successful clients are mostly those who use this process of explicating felt meanings *throughout* therapy. Clients who fail in therapy never refer to or employ felt meaning at all.

The findings say that focusing *is* an essential skill for getting out of emotional trouble if one is in trouble. This leads me to the conclusion that, if this is such an important skill, we ought to teach it in school—not just because it is creative thinking, but also because the same method (applied to personal feelings rather than intellectual reactions to subject matter) would enable people to resolve many of their personal conflicts—and to be more able to listen for felt meanings in those around them and aid them also. It seems quite a vital skill.

The Social Implications of Felt Meanings

Now I want to talk as a philosopher about meaning and science and the basic aims of education. If we grant the patient in psychotherapy the necessity of working with his felt meanings, of getting out of his construct-boxes, of moving not only with logical steps but also with steps through the complex felt concreteness, if we call anything less an ineffective way of being caught in conceptual boxes, in the happenstance of one's given assumptions and constructs—why then would we wish these severe limitations to remain in man's methods of thinking about man, about education, about society?

It is trite to say that our thinking about man and society has not kept pace with physics and natural science, that we must make comparable advances, really radical breakthroughs à la Galileo in our modes of thinking about the human world, otherwise our natural science advances may destroy us, and our calculating machines may exceed our human wisdom and may ruin us. We have given vast physical and mathematical powers into the keeping of a political and social system of power and education which has not advanced much in two thousand years of history.

Yet such a breakthrough in the human fields can only be of two sorts: either with or without our own personal humanness as individuals. If it will be without this, if there will eventually be a really successful and powerful science quite apart from your own and my own persons, your own and my own growth in regard to our human personal lives— if without this, then it cannot help but be a technology, a mechanized really nonhuman system working successfully enough apart from your and my life struggle not to need us, to run us without our living say-so. Such a science must make us less human (though perhaps more contented) and therefore it cannot be a science of humans as they really are. For to be human is to create meanings, values, problems, surprises even to ourselves. And so, it is a contradiction in terms (though realistically a possibility all the same) to hope for major scientific advance in the human fields without this involving the use of one's own personal living humanness.

Yet this means that, even though we may have given up in our own lives we must turn back from having turned back—we must hope to grasp the personal truths in our own struggles—we must use this superior method of thinking which employs our own felt meanings, even though in feelings are also our hurts, defeats, missed opportunities, and the sense of death soon to come. And, if I had somehow escaped these and been given everything I needed and all the luck and timely insight, then I should only have missed some of the complexity of felt life significance.

Why do I say all this? Because I am defending the new method of thinking against the charge that it is only as good as the individual person—this seems like its weakness. We are so used to a science that is independent of man, a science whose very basic constructs abstract the human element out, as though to assume as a basic principle of science that humans do not exist. We are so used to a science that does not need us—that consists only of conceptual structures perfectly represented on paper and capable of being fed into calculators without loss, whose implications are always only the necessary analytic mathematical ones so that no human felt sensing is needed.

But, even in physics this applies only to the finished product of science. In the making, science, discovery, new ideas, new hypotheses, new constructs, problem solving, all involve the kind of thinking I have described. Only the finished, precision product of physical science can stand alone without the felt sense of an individual.

There could not be a successful science in the human fields which would not use us as humans in its very method of thinking.

What is there in us which makes us so hesitant to confront our felt meanings and use them? What scares us so that we cling to our constructs only, that we find comfort in limiting ourselves to grinding out implications from given constructs only? I believe that it is our failures at living and the poor quality of the human being which we so often feel we really are, underneath. Yet this is no reason to turn away.

In class, in psychotherapy, in friendship, for example, what counts is not the quality of human being I am, or my wisdom. What counts is whether I will *be* a human being with people (if I will be a human being, I can only be the one I am, but fortunately this need not be so great or good or wise, it needs only to be a human being, and this we all are).

Similarly, in the new method of thinking one does not need one's feelings to be true or good or beautiful—the fuzzy feeling of some incipient thought I have need not be attractive-seeming nor after I explicate it does it need to turn out to be true. . . . I will soon change and modify and correct and test and rework it. My motives need not be pure. . . . I soon see the irrelevance of the irrelevant ones and how they block my further efforts to solve and resolve what still feels tense or fails to work in situations, and fails at its empirical tests. I soon create new constructs and work out their logic. I correct, elaborate, and fill in the breaks and the inconsistencies. But I can do it along new lines—lines that come from some felt aspects of my whole organically felt context instead of only the thin constructs I was given to begin with. All methods of logic and empirical testing in situations and research remain intact with this new method of thinking. Only, the original questions and constructs no longer need limit us. We can keep these and their implications but we can also create new ones, getting at new facets and formulating these in new constructs which lead to new implications and new variables and truths to test.

Measuring Felt Meanings

We used to think that this mode of thinking is "not measurable," that it is totally private, that we only hear and observe the conclusions and actions of a person, and cannot tell whether he arrived at these conclusions and actions through this sort of genuine thinking process, or some other way. This is not so. Today we have objective measures of the degree to which an individual employs his feeling process as a continual basis for his verbalizations and behavior.

Although the kind of thinking I refer to here is the same, there are many different kinds of situations in which we might want to measure it. Classrooms are different sorts of situations from therapy sessions, they have different specific aims, different kinds of behaviors appropriate to them, and hence the measures will have to be created anew for classrooms, even though we already have them for tape recorded psychotherapy.

The basic principle of these measures (rating scales, questionnaires, etc.) is to measure the kind of process going on rather than the kinds of content... *how* things are said and done, rather than *what* is said and done. For example: the sort of interaction between teacher and student, which I described and of which I said that it teaches this new kind of thinking (explicating the felt sense of thinking)... this kind of interaction can be observed and measured. However, it cannot be measured in terms of the content, of what is being said... because the same method can apply in any field, with any content. Nor can you get at it by counting the number of times the teacher asks questions, or answers questions, or presents factual material, or tries to get up discussion. For in all these different aspects of teaching there may be, or there may not be, the teacher's effort to pay attention to, to invite, to explicate, to go several steps with . . . the student's felt, as yet unformulated sense.

Felt Meaning as a Research Variable

How do we observe when an individual explicates his felt sense? We observe a search for words, we observe metaphorically novel ways of phrasing, we observe phrases that refer directly to something sensed (like "this thing" or "what I'm getting at" or "what puzzles me is, ah . . ." or "it's something like . . .", phrases which have no meaning whatever unless we accept them as pointers at something concretely there, felt, directly referred to by the individual within himself.

In research it is all-important, what variables you choose to define and measure. Good quantifying methods for tests, rating scales and questionnaries exist: many judges rating separately, one-way-vision glass, and tape recordings, many methods exist. In research we most often fail not for a dearth of methods but in the poor variables we first define.

From the things I have been saying two conclusions follow for the creation of research variables: First, let us define and measure the sorts of behaviors by teachers and students which I have been describing: the teacher's inviting and aiding students to explicate their felt—not yet explicit—thoughts and reactions, and the students' doing just that. Often this requires several steps of interchange and it is not at all difficult to notice (recall the rather characteristic descriptions I have given, which we all recognize).

Second, and more generally, you can take any interesting aspect of classroom behavior. As it is currently phrased, it is nearly always a *content* variable. You can convert it into a *process* variable (which, I think, will be much more likely to give you results). The procedure is as follows. Suppose you think you might take classroom interaction and divide the teacher's behaviors according to a classification system with variables like: asks question, presents information, approves student's speech, disapproves student's speech, gives instructions, etc. Now, my prediction is that one is most likely to find nothing with these variables. They concern *what* the teacher does. But, why then would one think of studying them? Because we may think that teachers who approve more, or who ask for discussion more, are more successful teachers.

We still think in terms of *what* is done. Let the next step be *why*. Why would one think that more approval makes better teaching? Because approval makes students more comfortable and hence more able to have and express their reactions and to think and learn. Then the third step is: that is a process variable: measure that directly. Always, your real and good reasons for being interested in the *content* variable will lead to an underlying *process* variable which can be measured directly.

For example, now that we want to measure students' freedom to have and express their reactions, we can set up various measures: a standard five-minute procedure in which a picture is shown by the teacher being tested, and the class is asked to describe it (or anything appropriate to the age and type of class, so long as it is a measure that will get at comfort-to-express. Hence it must be something to which anyone could have reactions he would like to express, not only bright children). Or, if you still want to classify teacher classroom behavior, you can now formulate a classification system that will really be relevant to what you want to measure: encouragement or discouragement of comfort-to-express.

You will be more concerned, now, with *different manners* in which material is presented, different manners in which questions are asked (rather than just whether material is presented *or* questions are asked). Is the material presented so that student-reactions to it can be appropriate? Is it presented whole—for comment, or cut up and only good for memorizing? Must student expressions be answers to questions only? Are questions sometimes directed at student reactions, or only to obtain student productions of correct answers?

From Content to Process

If we thought earlier that a large number of questions makes for discussion, we see now that our real interest lay in the kind of questions, in *how* questions were intended and posed. If, before, we thought large proportions of material-presenting behavior would be bad, we now realize we meant only a *manner* of presenting which precludes the student-expression we are interested in.

This, of course, is only an example, to illustrate that from any *content* variable that seems interesting we can move (via asking ourselves *why* it seems interesting) to the process variable which we really intend, and then we can measure it directly. (Of course, this requires devising a new instrument, a new rating scale, test situation or questionnaire, but the stage of development in our sciences about humans is such that, indeed, we usually must define new and more specific variables, categories and tests.)

Such instruments (for example, a rating scale used by several independent judges listening to tape recordings of classroom interaction) give us mathematical scores which we can then correlate with other measures, for example the number of failing grades or the number of dropouts or the increase over a year's period on intelligence tests, or any other measure you wish.

Transcending the Controversy between Content and Progressive Education

You will notice that I am proposing as worthwhile research variables (and as worthwhile aspects of practical teaching method) somewhat different issues than those argued about a few years ago in education. I am saying neither that there should be an intellectual emphasis (e.g., we need more physicists to catch up with the Russians) nor a personal adjustment emphasis (as in some extremes of progressive education). I am not saying that teachers should place emphasis on subject matter (though better quality performance by students on all subject matter is desirable) nor am I saying that teachers should drop the material they teach and become psychotherapists (though one must often respond to the child and not only to what he says).

I am not advocating the lecture method or the discussion method. We can move beyond these older divisions of viewpoint, to *more basic goals of education*. These older divisions are based on content, on *what* should be talked *about* and taught: should teacher and student talk about personal aspects or subject matter, should they talk about something the teacher brought up or something the student brought up, should there be more or less material presented by the teacher compared with the proportion given to student discussion? I am not talking about such questions of *what*, I am concerned with *how*.

It is true, with this new method of thinking as the basic "how" one cannot lecture *all the time*. However, it does not follow that one must never lecture. One should not force one's class structure on students without making room for and giving time to their reactions and to an explication of what it means to them, but it does not follow that a teacher must not impose any structure.

The underlying educational aim of those views that championed students' setting their own course of study and giving themselves their grades, the view which forbade lectures and the presentation of ordered material, which viewed it as a violation of freedom to give assignments or exams—the underlying educational aim of all that, was the student's developing his own process of thinking and inquiry. But we can hold to that principle without limiting what we do as teachers. The basic issue is not the assignment, but how it is given and used; not the grades but how they affect the nature of the whole course and class, not the teacher's presentation of ordered material but whether he does or does not then make room for steps of thought and explication as these occur in the student.

Years ago, before coming into a university I taught in a city college. Our students took printed city-wide exams mathematically graded. If I was not to cheat the students then it was my responsibility to give them the materials they would be tested on. I found that there was no contradiction between this and my other aims. I could present the material in ten minutes of each hour (our standards on content *are* too low!) and give the other forty minutes to the students' reactions and thinking about it. (Before I found this, I used to present my material, then ask for questions. No questions. So I would present it again, ask for questions, discuss with one or two bright students till the end of the hour, review the material again next time, and at mid-term and before the final. What a waste of time!) The basic principle of giving time to discussion is not a law against lectures, not that we must not present material in our own orderly way. The basic principle is that we must not keep the material *only* in the order and conceptual boxes in which we present it, but we must also teach the students to think on it, i.e., to move through their own steps (in orders and steps different from those our presentation implies); in short, that we help them think ... recognizing however that thinking is not only words and constructs but also felt sense and its explication.

Relevance to Experience

The controversy between content and progressive education can be resolved by being transcended. Progressive education (while my views probably come from some of its influence) is too often misunderstood as *content:* then it seems a de-emphasis of subject matter in favor of personal growth, play, unstructured classes, little real intellectual growth. It was not so intended. Rather, education must be viewed and studied as process—the kind of process going on in the student.

Aiding a student to explicate his felt sensing in thinking means aiding him to explicate his sense of the world and context he lives in, since that is what feeling and sensing is . . . our organic sentience of being bodily alive, interactively, in an environment. But this means that we must let the student live with, and interact with the actual subject matter so that it is part of the context in which he lives. This involves more and more direct, higher level subject matter, so that the student has a direct experiential sense of it. The teacher must not be the *only* one who really studies the subject matter directly—as it were, the teacher standing on a mountain from which he alone can see the real subject matter which he only reports indirectly in a secondhand and boiled down way to the students.

Some have tried to make this point by saying: make the class relevant to the student's "experience." Yet this is too often misunderstood to mean that you must bring the subject matter *down* to what the student has *already* experienced ... when it should mean, rather, that you must *extend* the student's experience so he experiences the subject matter! Thus higher intellectual quality, not boiling down, is implied in the new method.

As an illustration of the difference, consider the attempt to bring mathematics down to the student's "experience": mathematical problems are phrased in terms of "a boy goes to the store . . ." or "bags of brown candy and bags of red candy." To appeal to the student's experience of stores and candy does little for mathematics. What is really wanted is to extend the student's experiencing of mathematics (as the newer methods do, using rods of different length to teach quantitative relationships). The rods are tools: The point is not that rods can be experiences, but that with them there can be an experiencing of quantitative relationships. Thus, in mathematics we now extend the child's experience of the subject matter, so that the child does not have to learn by rote the steps of adding, then of subtracting, and so on, but can operate on his own with the directly experienced quantitative relationships of mathematics itself.

Similarly, in history, to bring it *down* to experience might be (when studying Lincoln) to remind students of who is on the penny, while to help them to *extend* their experience of history would involve marveling and puzzling (as historians do) over whether Lincoln could have avoided the war if he had been less stubborn . . . explicating the student's felt sensed reactions which then soon come to similar questions.

In conclusion, basic new trends of human thought are always fundamentally reflected in education—because education is the process of creating and fashioning human nature and society. In today's new trends of thought, the concrete experiential aspect is becoming more and more central. People used to think, centuries ago, that human nature was set and defined and they knew what it was (though they did not all agree, each group thought it knew). Human nature and reality seemed adequately dealt with in these, or those, constructs, definitions, concepts. Even in the nineteenth century, when so much cultural relativism and historicism showed the vast variety of what men can be and think—even then there were thought to be at least laws of history, of the historical evolution of cultures. But the 20th Century has seen us break all *forms:* in religion, in values, in how subject matter is presented, in social patterns of living, in non-Euclidean mathematics, in art.

Once forms have been broken through, once we see them as relative, we can no longer choose them as they were, absolutely and with seeming-organic solidity. They become *mere* forms and we must meet something else, something more. Experiential concreteness is not given in just one set of forms but it can always be carried forward, explicated and formed. A thinking which does that is a more powerful method of education, of psychotherapy, of human relations and of thinking generally, than any of the erstwhile absolute-seeming forms. Yet this method of proper interplay between felt concrete sensing and concepts is new.

We have only recently emerged from trends—in the first part of this century—in which this breakage of forms meant *either* a merely formal playing with these forms (a formal playing, logic-chopping, calculus-making, which was possible just because the forms had been pulled away from concreteness and shown to be so easily variable), *or* a glorification of the emotional, the merely felt and unexplicated, the ambiguous, ephemeral and unspeakable (again that sort of view was possible only because forms had been pulled off and had been found so variable). Thus there was Logical Positivism and Existentialism in philosophy, intellectual and personality emphases in education; and in society on the one hand an increasing technologizing abstracted from one's being human, and on the other hand an increasing emphasis on psychotherapy and the emotional needs of this individual human who now had to live in a more and more complex, rationalized, social system which was more and more swiftly changing and variable, no longer organically embodied in his living identity, as preindustrial social forms had been.

If you consider feeling and form as two static entities, then the split is devastating: it results in unexamined inexplicit blind emotionality (be it beautiful or Nazi-like) on the one hand, and mere formalism on the other side. Yet if we take these two, not as static, if in thinking and explication they are in motion, each carrying the other forward, then this modern relativity of all values and forms will have given birth to a new and much more powerful method of human thinking in the sciences about man, as well as in living socially and individually, in how we deal with ourselves and our feelings, and in our thinking about education as well as in our practical procedures and research variables.

References

Eugene T. Gendlin. *Experiencing and the Creation of Meaning.* New York: Free Press, 1962.

Eugene T. Gendlin. "A Theory of Personality Change." Chapter in: *Personality Change.* Philip Worchel and Donn Byrne, editors. Symposium on Personality Change, University of Texas. New York: John Wiley & Sons, Inc., 1964.

What Language Reveals

Walter Loban

LANGUAGE is the base of almost all modern education. Below this language base one finds not subjects for instruction but the bedrock itself—human perception, emotion, volition and thought. But these four are, in themselves, mere energies without direction. Perceiving, feeling, willing and thinking are shaped through language and action. Through language and action they are given form and design, thereby gaining meaning and significance. Language and action, these are the two crucial ways of educating mankind. Of the two, language gains in importance as any culture or nation moves from primitive to civilized conditions.

Although we will here discuss only one of the two, *language,* I wish to comment briefly on the other, *action,* or as it is sometimes phrased, *experience.* Modern societies have never fully envisioned the educational uses of experience and as a result our schools remain excessively verbal in their emphasis and incomplete in their accomplishments. Crucially important though language is, especially for developing the powers of reasoning, language is nevertheless limited in its powers to educate. The time must come when schools develop the full range of human experience. In future schools, outdoor camping will appear often in the curricula of younger pupils; art, music, drama and the dance will assume their important central roles for everyone; older pupils will design, build, decorate and sell houses and machines; work experience will be a part of general education and travel will not be an unusual educational event. Future pupils will learn much through experience, much that cannot be fully conveyed by words alone, and language will often be linked to experience.

Nevertheless words are of immense importance. Through language an individual classifies the objects and experiences he encounters, and through language he relates these perceptions as well as stabilizes them sufficiently to control them or to adapt to them. The climb from concrete objects to abstract concepts is slow for everyone, yet through language individuals can achieve this climb, reaching a better equilibrium and organization of their inner and their outer worlds. Language, therefore, reveals much that is crucial to education.

In this paper, what language reveals will be organized under three headings:

What language reveals about people

What language reveals about itself

Teaching pupils to use language effectively.

For the first two of these categories only an overview will be given; the scholarship about language and its anthropological implications constitutes an enormous library by itself. Nevertheless something of what language reveals about people and about itself is necessary for reviewing what teachers should do with it in schools.

What Language Reveals About People

The language an individual uses reflects the social and geographical background of his living. Has he migrated from one nation to another? His language will always retain some hint of a foreign rhythm. Has he come from a certain geographical area? His Texan English, his Gascogne French or his Venetian Italian will show his origins. Equally noticeable is the language of his social group. It may be that he does not speak the prestige dialect—one of the varieties of standard American English or Parisian French or Castilian Spanish. He may reveal himself as a member of a minority, usually one of a class of persons not sharing the satisfactions and privileges of those who speak the standard language. Or he may belong to some special group such as teen-agers in all urban cultures, gypsies in Sweden, or beatniks in our own country. "He doesn't talk like us" is equivalent to saying "He isn't one of us," and language reveals much about a person's kind of living and position in the large society.

Language is also a means by which human infants are socialized and thus language becomes a potent symbol of social solidarity. Schools in democracies seek or should seek to open the doors of achievement and fulfillment to all pupils, but sometimes the school, more often the community, diminishes such opportunities. Language is one of the major ways in which this process of social control operates. Here it is important to remember that language is learned in one's family and group. Only by actually being among those who speak differently does anyone modify his language. Traditional instruction, exhortation and drills are not enough. If minority groups who speak differently are to be drawn into the mainstream of a nation's life, they must not attend schools where they are grouped by themselves; rather they and their families must enter all social and economic spheres of living. Language is thus an important means of social class solidarity and adjustment to social necessity.

Those whose lives relate to complex and abstract thought develop the most effective uses of language complexity. Those who dwell in slum or pioneer conditions often find language less useful than action. Juvenile gangs and antisocial leatherjacketed motorcyclists do not talk out their problems; they act out their problems. Those who occupy the least favored economic positions of a nation are mainly (and understandably) concerned with the immediate present; they seldom use language to examine the past or to anticipate the future. They do not verbalize the nuances of subjective feeling, and their lives orient them to descriptive rather than analytical uses of language. As a result their language, in comparison to that of more favored social groups, employs fewer complex sentences, subordinate clauses, infinitive and participial phrases, nominative absolutes, appositives—all those devices most effective speakers use to show distinctions and precise relationships.

To those whose language is restricted, people such as teachers sound very prolix, very "talky," and in school their children find themselves puzzled by so much strange talk. For self-respect such children often turn back to their own group, reject the school, and become problems until they drop out. Valuable and comforting though their own social group and language may be, such children have missed an opportunity to learn those forms of language which enable an individual to think precisely and to cope more effectively with his environment. The fault is not, of course, theirs, nor is the school always lacking in desire to help. Nevertheless, much could yet be done in education to induct such children less traumatically and more gradually into a fuller use of the potential of language. There is nothing in the basic structures of their language to prevent their learning the ways of elaborating those structures to express more complex ideas. However, they will not elaborate the sentence structures they know unless life at home or in school makes it important and desirable to do so.

If language reveals much about social groups, it reveals much about individuals, too. It reflects their view of themselves and their personal security with others. People who have power over spoken language are typically those who feel secure, are at ease with other people, respecting themselves and others, and therefore able to speak easily and sincerely. They have the flexibility and resiliency deriving from a realization that the world is complicated and that there are no simple solutions for most problems; they are sensitive to other people and perceive how others receive what they say. They use the prevailing language conventions of the community in which they live, enunciate clearly, use a pleasant tone of voice, and speak with reasonable fluency. Although this is not always true, they are frequently the ones who can adapt their language to different listeners.

Such individuals usually come from backgrounds of aspiration and are open to and interested in experience. Vitality, wisdom, integrity and courage manifest themselves in oral language, and the ability to speak easily and well has deep connections with one's security and self-image. Insecure people often talk either too much or too little. They, too, are trying to adjust to their environment, and language or silence is their attempt. Violent dogmatism, false humility, smugness, and snobbery are typical of other undesirable personal factors that show up in vocabulary, style, diction and tone. Thus, schools cannot do much with language apart from a concern with the child's self-image.

About human worth, however, language reveals nothing. Individual worth and dignity cannot be estimated by the dialect or manner of speech a man uses. Many admirable people of noble behavior lack the educated language ease of typical community leaders and do not necessarily speak the prestige dialect.

What Language Reveals About Itself

It is an interesting historical fact that mankind has been slow to apply the methods of science to language. Apparently man had to observe the stars and fix his course on desert or sea before he could turn much of his attention to the phenomenon of self. Astronomy was followed by other sciences. In our own time anthropology has led us to the beginnings of a scientific study of language. We realize now that language is a *system,* that it is a system of *arbitrary* voice signals, that it is essentially *speech.* Writing is a way of reproducing speech, but no written language exists unless there is first a spoken language. We know also that *language changes,* the sounds and words more rapidly than the system, and that all languages communicate by utterances using subjects and predication about those subjects. Most important of all, we know that language and thinking are closely interlocked.[1]

Language and thinking are interrelated by virtue of the fact that human language is composed of symbols. A fundamental difference between the animal and the human world is linguistic. Animals can use and understand cues; they cannot cope with symbols. A growl, a call, even a green traffic light—cues like these, directly tied to a concrete situation, can take on meaning for animals as well as for human beings. Symbols, however, are instruments of complicated thought. They are not necessarily tied to the immediate situation, for by means of symbols human beings can allude to objects or concepts even in the absence of those objects or concepts.

This language system is amazingly flexible. It can be enlarged to name new concepts, such as *camouflage* in 1918, *jet plane* in 1960, and *cosmonaut* in 1967. Also, the individual symbols in the system can be used for more than one symbolization. Response to any linguistic symbol is contingent upon the symbols with which it is combined. For instance, in English-speaking communities, response to the symbol *crop* differs in the following four sets of utterances because of the surrounding symbols:

The stone stuck in the bird's *crop*.

She carried a riding *crop* in her hand.

The shepherd watched his sheep *crop* the grass.

The farmer reaped a *crop* of barley.

The cues used by animals never become language for discourse because animals are incapable of separating the cues from the particular concrete situations in which cues are embedded. No evidence of animals having made the leap from cues to symbolic language, to words freed from situations and arranged in systems of contingency has ever been verified.[2] Until the day she learned w a t e r as a symbol, and thereby *disassociated the symbol from any particular wetness*, Helen Keller lived the life of a gifted animal using cues. On that day, in a spectacular leap, she extended her potential limits to the mental horizon of the human family. Human beings use cues, of course, but they also use

[1] See *Harvard Educational Review* 34 (2): 354; Spring 1964.

[2] A summary of research on behavior in animals in relation to language may be found in Roger Brown. *Words and Things*. Glencoe, Illinois: The Free Press, 1958. See chapter V, "The Comparative Psychology of Linguistic Reference," p. 155-93.

symbols. Without symbolic language there would be no formation of concepts, no dominance of abstract knowledge over concrete knowledge. Without symbolic language, there would be no civilization, no passing on of cultures.

There are many ways of thinking with language symbols, ways that need to be part of every child's education. Thinking with language, he can classify into categories, comparing and contrasting, making subtle distinctions. He can deduce and induce. He can generalize. He can see relationships and he can reason by analogy. He can also dream and imagine and make intuitive leaps in the dark. He can unify his thoughts by imposing either a rational or an imaginative design upon the content of his thought. The language of uneducated men is distinguished from the language of educated men by the greater disjunction and separation in the component parts of whatever they wish to communicate. There is in their language a lack of that "prospectiveness of mind, that *surview*, which enables a man to foresee the whole of what he is to convey; and by this means so to subordinate and arrange the different parts according to their relative importance, in order to convey it as an organized whole."[3]

Another aspect of language that education can use more fully may be called the two countenances of language. Language can be shaped toward objective, dispassionate referential use, as science and mathematics do. Or language can be bent toward subjective, vivid emotive use, as literature does. Through scientific language we *understand;* through literary language we *realize*. Both forms—and their mixtures in everyday discourse—reveal much about how language is related to thinking and feeling. Both forms are important to man and need to be taught as a part of education.

Language has its limits, nevertheless, and beyond language lie ways of expressing what exists within the potential of man which cannot be communicated through grammatical discourse. Music, art and dance release these ineffable feelings and concepts, and literature, too, although anchored in the grammar of a language, transcends discourse to become an art and communicate through aesthetic modes.

Teaching Pupils To Use Language Effectively

What language reveals about people and about its own nature can be used in helping schools teach pupils a more effective use of language. To begin a consideration of language and education, we will look more closely at the problem of social class dialect.

[3] Samuel Taylor Coleridge, *Biographia Literaria.*

Because his oral language is such an important part of the child's connection with his home and social group and because it is the most important resource available to the school for educating the child, teachers should not inhibit the primary school child by criticizing his language. Here, then, is the place to begin helping pupils whose indigenous language differs from that of the larger community. A sequential language curriculum would have these strategies for pupils who speak a social class dialect or non-standard English:

1. Start these pupils earlier than others by giving them selected experiences in prekindergarten, experiences selected by virtue of their necessity in forming concepts needed for school work.

2. Educate teachers, both in-service and preservice, in the true nature of language. Many teachers still have the knowledge of quack doctors in this field.

3. In the kindergarten and earliest years of school, the emphasis should be upon the child's using *whatever language he already has* as the means of thinking, exploring, imagining and expressing. If he does not speak the prestige dialect, he can begin to link language with thinking and perceiving, using his own dialect. At this stage it is much too early to press him to use standard English; such mistaken teaching merely confuses the child and causes him to speak less in school.

4. In the primary school the teacher will begin to introduce many listening experiences in which very brief lively stories or riddles occur in two versions: one in standard English and one in the dialect familiar to the child. No invidious distinctions need be drawn, but the children will have their attention focused upon *listening for the differences.* The child needs to imitate all the phonemes of the standard dialect while he is still young and linguistically flexible. These skits may be live, they may be on records or on tapes with listening post arrangements.

5. In the upper years of the elementary school the teachers will take a further step: they will have the children further *imitate* many ways of speaking English, again in skits, brief and lively. Popular songs with many varieties of English—Scotch, Cockney, Cajun, Pidgin, Pennsylvania Dutch, Appalachian, Lancashire, Southern Negro, British, Australian—will be heard and sung. The teachers will also begin to provide guidance in oral usage of such noticeable items as *ain't* and the *double negative.* Usage (not grammar) will be taught *orally through imitation and listening practice.*

6. At some point, grades six or seven, the facts about standard and non-standard language will need to be explained by teachers whose own security and wisdom enable them to know that standard English is only a prestige dialect and that human worth has nothing to do with language. The pupils will be helped to see that there is nothing wrong with the dialect they and their parents use, but that economic and social penalties will be exacted of them if they cannot handle both forms of the language. Standard ways of speaking are like standard light bulb sockets, an efficient convenience. Social studies teachers will also deal with language as a social force, noting its social role. Also beginning at this time and lasting until graduation pupils will study language as content, that is, the miracle of language, looking at the fascinating ways of symbols and cues, how neighboring words change word meanings, the reasons for language change and for dialect, the regional varieties of speech, the *true* grammatical structure of English, the social aspects that lie back of usage, the dangers of perjury, propaganda, and a myriad of other interesting facets of language. Pupils will be led to note that newspapers, texts, newscasts are in standard English and why.

7. Throughout the entire years of a pupil's schooling there will be many occasions when teachers read aloud, fine speakers are heard on recordings, and successful guest speakers of many different ethnic backgrounds talk to the pupils. Drama and poetry will be used more often, and tape recorders will be in all classrooms.

8. Curricula will include more attention to *oral* language and *oral language will be evaluated on tests of achievement.*

9. Teachers will be selected for their understanding of the truths about language, not for an illiberal adherence to so-called "correct speech" improperly understood.

10. Implementing all this will require class size in the 20's rather than 30's or 40's. And, lest we anticipate Utopia, all these changes will undoubtedly bring some new problems as we solve the old problems. Education is never perfected.

11. Junior and senior high school classes will use language laboratory aural-oral approaches to drill for those who are still learning standard ways of speech.

Persistently through all of this, teachers will help pupils to elaborate their kernel sentences in order to express complex and useful ideas. Manipulation of sentences, not grammar, will be the method. From my own research I know that the difference between effective and non-effective users of language does not appear in their control of the grammatical sentence patterns, for all pupils know these before they enter school. Not grammatical sentence patterns but what is done to achieve greater flexibility and modification of ideas within these patterns proves to be the real measure of proficiency with language.[4]

Since formal instruction in grammar—whether linguistic or traditional—has not yet proved to be an effective method of *improving expression*, one can conclude that pupils need many opportunities to grapple with their own thought and express it in situations where they have someone to whom they wish to communicate successfully. Instruction can best aid the pupils' expression when individuals or small groups with similar problems are helped to see how *their own* expression can be improved. This instruction would take the form of identifying elements which strengthen or weaken communication, increase or lower precision of thought, clarify or blur meanings. For the pupils the approach will usually be through listening to and imitating models, through meaning and reasoning rather than through drills and the application of grammatical rules. In the early years, children might practice sentence manipulation by carrying placard words to the front of the room and then arranging and rearranging themselves to form variations of the sentences their placard words express. The chalk board and flannel board, too, offer similar possibilities for getting a preliminary kinesthetic feel for sentence manipulation. Next, word cards and linguistic blocks for seat work and the opaque projector can provide the same approach to manipulation of sentences. Finally they will work on their own compositions and oral discussions.

The persistently parallel relation of language proficiency with socio-economic status cannot be overlooked. It appears entirely possible that, much more than previously thought, language proficiency may be environmentally as well as hereditarily determined. If children reared in families at the least favored socioeconomic positions receive a restricted

[4] Walter Loban. *Language Ability: Grades Seven, Eight, and Nine.* Office of Education, U.S. Department of Health, Education, and Welfare. Washington, D.C.: U.S. Government Printing Office, 1966.

————. *The Language of Elementary School Children.* NCTE Research Report No. 1; Champaign, Illinois: National Council of Teachers of English, 1963.

————. "Language Proficiency and School Learning." In *Learning and the Educational Process,* John D. Krumboltz, editor. Chicago, Illinois: Rand McNally and Company, 1965, p. 113-31.

————. *Problems in Oral English.* NCTE Research Report No. 5. Champaign, Illinois: National Council of Teachers of English, 1966.

language experience at home, if their early linguistic environment stresses only limited features of language potential, such children will indeed be at a disadvantage in school and in the world beyond school—unless the school offers a planned sequential program of language instruction.

Those subjects most proficient with language are the ones who most frequently use language to express tentativeness. Supposition, hypothesis, and conditional statements occur much less frequently in the spoken language of those lacking skill in language. Teachers can help with this by asking more questions that begin with *why, what if, suppose that,* and fewer questions beginning with *what* and *when.*[5]

From all this we can realize that the child's self-image, his feeling toward the teacher, and his relationships with the other children in the school constitute additional factors that will shape the style and fluency of his language. On this matter, there are no easy educational guides. Everything that is done to give a human kind of striving-quality to learning and schooling will help to give the individual that self-respect and assurance making for better control of language in one's reactions with other people.

We can also see that much more needs to be done to link language with thinking. Teachers who are aware of the importance of inductive thinking, the usefulness of categories, the power of analogies, and what it means to generalize will be teachers who are more likely to elicit language for such purposes. Not WHAT and WHEN but rather SUPPOSE THAT . . . WHAT IF? . . . WHY? . . . will be the approach of teachers in all areas of the curriculum, not just in language arts or English.

Inasmuch as language is essentially oral, schools will give more attention to oral language—not, of course, encouraging mere talk and chatter but rather emphasizing what might be called thinking on one's feet, learning to organize ideas in group discussion, to cleave to the heart of a topic, to make progress with ideas and to generalize when enough illustrations have been given. Pupils in such situations will learn how to retreat gracefully from untenable positions, to be tentative but forceful in presenting ideas, to welcome differences of opinion, and to realize that one should have the courage to present minority opinion so that the group may have access to all sides of an issue.

Finally, curriculum directors and supervisors will need to aid teachers in developing adequate means of evaluating growth in oral skill, for until anything is evaluated it is unlikely to receive much emphasis

[5] Walter Loban. *The Language of Elementary School Children.* NCTE Research Report No. 1. Champaign, Illinois: National Council of Teachers of English (508 South Sixth Street), 1963.

in the curriculum. "Give me the power to evaluate and I will control the curriculum" is a memorable saying. The boundaries of the curriculum inevitably shrink to whatever is evaluated and at the present time oral proficiency, the base of almost everything discussed in this paper, is scarcely evaluated at all. With modern recording devices, teachers are now able to evaluate oral language and there is at last an excellent chance of improvement in oral language instruction, an improvement that will ultimately prove to be more valuable to education than all that has happened in science, mathematics, and foreign language instruction.

Through experience and through language we learn.

Experience needs language to give it form.

Language needs experience to give it content.

Learners need to be open to experience, to live fully, and to arrange, shape, and clarify their experience by expressing it in effective language. Here is the base of all true education, whether in school or in all of life.

Meaning and Thinking

Mary Jane McCue Aschner

THERE seems to be almost no limit to what we can consider relevant to the topics of meaning and thinking from the standpoint of the interests and concerns of the educator. Therefore it is necessary to take a sufficiently narrow line of approach to these matters in order to come out in the end with some kind of meaning for our thinking that will have practical import for our tasks of educating America's children.

Out of the boundless realms of what can be meant by "meaning," I shall examine two modes or aspects of meaning that seem to have direct bearing upon thinking in relation to its role in equipping the well-developed intelligence for effective action. One of these I call *"attached meaning"* and the other, *"addressed meaning."* In defining these terms, I shall try to clarify what I have in mind and to explain why I believe these two modes of meaning are basic to the development of thinking abilities as an educational objective.

It is the plan of this paper to begin with some considerations of how meaning and thinking become so important in the tenure of mankind on this earth. From this I shall describe and illustrate the two modes of meaning already noted. Following, there will be a presentation and discussion of some conceptions or models of thinking that have practical relevance to classroom practice. In concluding, some fairly concrete suggestions will be made about how teachers may go about putting these ideas to work.

It could be claimed that meaning—however one conceives it for the moment—has become man's specialty. Man is a constant seeker after meaning, a maker of meaning, and a wielder of meaning in the pursuit of his own ends. Meaninglessness stands synonymous with despair in the hearts of many, and in the chilly regard of the disenchanted ones as the actualization of man's final absurdity. But educators are rarely among the disenchanted ones; they are seldom cast down in despair, though they often live in days of desperation. Fundamentally educators are optimists, and they are convinced that their life and work are truly meaningful.

Man and Meaning in Evolution

When did man begin? Perhaps one good answer to this question is the proposition that man began when he became directly concerned with the meaning of things. Aeons beyond reckoning in the past, some primate probably took his first stride toward becoming human when he began to *consider* his situation in the light of its possible import for him. That was the moment when this bright anthropoid started coping with the problem of survival by reflection rather than mere reaction. In this moment, he stopped to examine the "givens" in his present plight in terms of what they might mean—*signify* or *portend*— for his chances of staying alive. And he explored these "givens" (we call them data of "information input") for whatever meaning they might hold—*suggest* or *indicate*—regarding alternative courses of action. When this kind of thinking went to work, the survival quotient of the being who began it, and that of all his kith and kin, took a rapid rise upward.

Reflective thinking, as briefly sketched in here, involves some processes that seem to set man apart from his fellow primates. To reflect on things, after all, is to act mentally, and at the moment at least, independently of physical action. Such thinking also involves not only keeping several things in mind at the same time, but manipulating them in some systematic way. Man thinks about the possibilities for action and explores their probable consequences; he measures possibilities and probabilities in the light of his present situation and of his present and ultimate purpose. This entails perspective—the capacity to take the long-term view of things as well as the short-term view. This capacity to think reflectively and systematically equips one to be a decision maker and a planner. This is one of our distinguishing characteristics as human beings—our capacity to decide and to plan on the basis of reflection.

It may be at this point that we moved ahead of the chimps. But here someone may remind us of the remarkable accomplishments of Sultan, Köhler's famous gifted chimp (see Wolfgang Köhler's *The Mentality of Apes*, 1925). After all, Sultan was certainly capable of sizing up a situation accurately and of taking intelligent action. That is, he could put two and two together (two lengths of bamboo) and solve his problem efficiently by hauling in that distant delectable banana. So we must grant that Sultan could scan his situation, and act successfully to accomplish his purpose. So far what separates us from the chimps? Certainly not the ability to do problem-solving jobs well. But was Sultan a planner? Did he plan for future banana problems? No, it seems he never made that step ahead. Granted, he was a shrewd mechanic, a true maker of implements and tools, as are many of his kind. But here is where Sultan and his kind left off, and we took the next step ahead.

This big step was taken by one of our ancestors when he began devoting a considerable portion of his time and energies to the making of tools and other kinds of implements, such as clay containers for food and liquids. For in the design and manufacture of implements, plans and provisions for the future are made. Who would bother making a spare spear if he did not anticipate a future need? Perhaps we owe this first specialized tool-maker a hearty vote of thanks. For in directing his thought and efforts toward planning for his own future, he made our appearance on the scene a part of that future.

The role of language must also be considered for its bearing on the evolution of human intelligence. It has been claimed that man did not progress beyond the level of his fellow primates until the advent of language, and that it was his achievement of language which put man finally into the lead. Yet recent studies by paleontologists and anthropologists now indicate that man made his first major move forward well *before* the invention of language as we now know it (Spuhler, 1959). This big step was taken when man turned in earnest to the job of making implements as a means of providing for and planning for the future.

The other primates, though they learned to make and use tools to obtain food, for example, never devoted serious consideration to the possible advantages of making and stock-piling implements as a specialized way of dealing with the environment. Chimps can consider the "givens" about them, and make something do as a tool to obtain the desired object of the moment. But they never quite got to the point of seeing to making itself as a generalized instrumental goal for managing things to come. Maybe it was man's ability to *think ahead*, and the chimp's inability to do this that separated us once and for all from our fellow primates.

It is this kind of "thinking ahead" that is evidenced in the enterprise of making tools that probably enabled man to achieve the level of control over his environment that made language the next necessary tool, for man's environment expanded with the extension of his control over it. He began coping with the problems of survival—food gathering, shelter, and defense—through cooperation with other men. And a cooperative endeavor demands communication among those involved. Yet in view of all this, it is fair to say that our capacity for reflective thinking scarcely surpassed Sultan's level of problem solving until we had made of language our most effective instrument of thought.

Two Basic Modes of Meaning

When we consider meaning in terms of its origins in relation to the ability to think, it becomes obvious that there is one very important kind of meaning—so far as effective thinking is concerned—that is not related to or dependent upon the kind of meaning we associate with language and verbal behavior. This is a form of "preverbal" meaning; it is not man's special province—other species deal with this mode of meaning in their efforts to understand and cope with the environment.

Yet it would be the worst kind of nonsense to conclude that, since this *preverbal* domain of meaning figures importantly in the lives of creatures lower than we on the evolutionary ladder, it is not as important a contributor to our thinking as the kind of meaning that is related to language. Intelligent problem solving, decision making, and planning depend upon the effectiveness with which we deal with both modes of meaning.

Attached Meaning

For purposes here, the *preverbal* mode of meaning is called attached meaning. It is the significance and the import that is attached or ascribed to certain features of the immediate situation in which one finds oneself. Attached meaning has to do with how we classify the data received through our perception of the situation with "what we make" of the informational input. This is meaning brought to the situation by the individual, and which he attaches to such features of the environment that stand out—that impinge upon his awareness—as he perceives his situation. One's perceptions are not only determined by his present purposes, but also by the kinds of experiences and attitudes he brings to the present situation (Bruner, 1957). Most specifically this mode of meaning is distinguished from others by virtue of the fact that no agent or agency sent or addressed the meaning to the individual. It is mainly his interpretation that shapes the meaning of things for the individual. This of course holds also for what meaning one makes of the mode (speech, writing, gestures) in which someone has addressed him. But the major point here is that meaning is made out of what is "there" that was not intended to be sent forth by or from its perceived source. The source of such meaning may be inert and inanimate, or it may be animate and active. But the how and the why of its meaning depend more upon its beholder than upon its own nature.

Take the meaning of a mountain peak, for example. To the alpinist it may mean a challenge to his daring that he purposes to meet. He plans to scale the peak, or else! To the alpine guide, the same peak may mean no challenge at all, but only a somewhat tiring means by which to earn a living from the tourists. To the poet, this peak may mean something he expresses in writing of "sermons in stone." And the painter may see it as the meaning of remote grandeur epitomized, now to be captured on canvas.

Consider another situation involving mountains, and what most of us call "natural signs" that something is going to happen. Take the caveman and his modern descendant, the sportsman deer hunter. Uncounted millenia apart in time, these two individuals may very well *attach* the same meaning to the same event: the sudden turmoil of darkening, gathering storm clouds, near the saddle ridge below the peak, toward which each—in his own time—is heading. Both men "see" these cloud-gatherings as meaning "rain soon, and probably a big storm." Both may decide on the basis of this interpretation to take the same kind of action. Og heads back for the cave, and Ogden beats it back down the slope to his car and heads for home.

Even commonly interpreted "natural signs" can mean different things to different people. Consider the case of Herr Alpenfels, a small farmer and sage of this district. He is especially famed as a weather prophet. He scans the same skies, viewing them from the same general position as that from which Og and, some time later, our contemporary Ogden looked up and saw these signs as meaning—*portending* or *signifying*—the imminent onslaught of a rainstorm. But old farmer Alpenfels sizes up the situation quite differently. Sniffing the wind and testing its direction with a wet finger, Herr Alpenfels concludes that this is just the prelude to a storm that will not break till tomorrow. So he predicts "rain tomorrow" from the meaning he has attached to the same sky conditions that meant "rain right soon" to others. Farmer Alpenfels acts differently, too, on the basis of his interpretation of what the storm clouds signified to him. He has decided to leave his cattle up on the high alm for the night and bring them down before noontime next day, giving them that much more time to graze the fresh grasses of his meadow land.

People are part of our environment, too. Sometimes we *attach* meaning to what they do, or do not do, or say or do not say. But again, our ascription of meaning is still mostly a matter of our own doing, unless the other person or persons in our situation are explicitly addressing their words or their actions to us. Consider the case of the mother busy in her kitchen who becomes aware of a striking silence in the playroom, where her two children have been heard playing and prattling steadily for some time. And now this long, noticeable silence. "What is going on?" wonders Mother. To her the unexpected silence suggests several possibilities, not all of them welcome! The children have moved from the playroom to some other place out of earshot; they are tired and have dropped off to sleep (unlikely, she muses); or they are up to some kind of mischief. She decides to act on the basis of the possible meanings of silence when silence signifies for her that something unusual is going on. So she goes to investigate. Much to her surprise, both youngsters have fallen sound asleep.

The silence signified *something*, as we have noted, but it was not a message from children to mother. Nor would the silence itself have consisted in a message sent to mother even if the children had carefully plotted silence just in order to lure Mother into the playroom in order to play a trick on her. In that event, the children would have manipulated the situation on the basis of their ability to predict how Mother would interpret it, and how she would then act on her interpretation. They did not address their mother; they simply rigged the situation so that she would read into it a certain meaning and subsequently take action.

People often tend to interpret others' behavior as if it were intended for them to "receive." For example, the social studies teacher has just begun an explanation of some historical issue that was raised by one of the students in the current discussion. In the back of the room sit Nancy and Linda. Both are apparently listening attentively to the teacher's remarks. Suddenly Nancy frowns and shakes her head, her eyes still on the teacher. Then she turns and whispers something to Linda.

From the teacher's point of view, it seems quite clear that some part of her explanation has provoked Nancy to disagree with her, and then to act rudely in turning to whisper to Linda. From the teacher's standpoint, this interpretation of Nancy's action, as directed initially to her in an expressed negation of something, is perfectly plausible. Other observers might also interpret Nancy's behavior as intended to express some kind of negative response to the teacher's remarks. But it does not necessarily follow that what looks like "meant" behavior is in fact "meant" to express anything to anyone.

For example, in this case, the teacher's use of the word "labor" in discussing labor and management relations is what brought the frown to Nancy's face. All day long she has been worried about her mother who is in labor at this very moment to deliver a new baby. Nancy has kept in touch with her father at the hospital by telephone. Just before class Dad had said it would be "any minute now." Nancy has been trying to concentrate on class discussion to keep her mind off her worry and fears for her mother. But that word "labor," uttered in quite a different context of thought, brought her mother's plight vividly back to mind. Her frown was a reaction to her own thoughts, and was in no way a response to the teacher. Her whispers to Linda were not about the teacher or what she had said. Nancy was telling Linda that she did not see how she could stand it any longer—she was going to leave after this class and rush to the hospital, no matter what the principal might do to her.

Granted, this is a rather dramatic example of how meaning can be attached to behavior on the assumption that the behavior was addressed to its interpreter by the person observed. Here the assumption was mistaken; no message was meant for anyone by the frown and the shaking of a head. (After all, such gestures and expressions do conventionally express meaning.) This confusion of interpretation can cause teachers much trouble. It is important to observe behaviors in the classroom, and it is equally if not more important to avoid hasty interpretations. This is true because our actions are in all cases based on the meaning we see in a situation. Yet it is unwise to read into a situation what in fact may not be there at all, and then worse still, to judge someone (a mental action) mistakenly on the basis of that misinterpretation.

Addressed Meaning

A second mode of meaning that has so much to do with thought and action consists in what we do in our efforts to communicate with others. We address (send) some "message" that we intend for some other person or persons (and some of our animal friends, too) to receive, to "take in." Normally we intend to communicate what we have in mind in such a way that it will be understood *as meant*—so that our addressee, so to speak, will comprehend accurately what we are trying to tell him. (Of course we also tell lies and sometimes deliberately "encode" our message so that it will be taken in a way that is misleading to its recipient; we may appear to mean one thing—e.g., friendly candor—when in fact our purpose is to disarm the other fellow in order to obtain information he might be otherwise reticent to impart.)

Actions that are carried out in order to communicate are both the vehicle and the embodiment of addressed meaning. We communicate by using symbols, by writing and speaking, and by making certain kinds of physical movements—gestures, expressions of feeling by face and eyes, hands and body—that we use to convey certain meanings according to the conventions in force within a given social group, community, or culture. Whatever kind of communication we use, it is shaped by convention—often by unwritten "ground rules" that determine *how* we can say or tell something to someone. Moreover, and equally important, communication is to be understood as a form of action, not merely as its product or "content." As addressed action, meaning has its agent, its intent, and its "target" or intended recipient.

Using Symbols To Mean

One of our most common nonverbal forms of communication involves the use of symbols. These can be lights, shapes, sounds, code systems, emblems, signs, and of course many other things. Thus the bell buoy warns the ship away from the shoals, the beacon fire hails the rescuers in their nighttime search for marooned mountain climbers; the siren warns of approaching retribution (traffic cops), announces the lunch hour, proclaims the advent of destruction by bombing, or clears the road for an ambulance or a fire engine. Red, yellow and green traffic lights govern our stops and starts on the streets; the curved arrow on the road sign informs us of a sharp curve ahead.

The chalkboard teems with the sprawling cryptic code—systems of symbols that mathematicians and scientists use in thinking their way through theoretical problems. The score of a Mozart symphony tells the conductor when to raise his baton as a signal to the woodwinds section to take up their melodic dialogue with the strings. All these are effective acts of communication, addressed, hopefully understood, and yielding some kind of response (not necessarily overt or in direct reply).

Though symbols used in communication do not depend on "worded" language, and their range of use is more limited, still there are some ways of communicating that cannot be better achieved by any other means.

Using Words and Sentences To Mean

Verbal communication is surely one of man's most complex and highly developed forms of social and intellectual activity. There is so much more meaning involved in communication between individuals and groups than what naively is supposed to reside in words and sentences, as the supposed containers and conveyors of meaning.

Let me underscore again the action aspect of verbal behavior as activity that *is* meaning by citing the late philosopher Ludwig Wittgenstein, whose intent it was ". . . to bring into prominence the fact that the speaking of language is part of an activity, or of a form of life" (1953, p. 11). The rest of that activity or form of life to which Wittgenstein referred consists mainly in what I have referred to as communication in and through the addressing, receiving and responding actions that in themselves constitute meaning. The meanings of words consist in our use of them, what we do with them, and how we handle them within a given context or situation.

We do many different kinds of things in our verbal activities. In Wittgenstein's listing of some of these activities, notice how many involve many kinds of thinking, and how many of these verbal activities, or "language games" are a regular feature of everyday life in the classroom. (Wittgenstein was himself a schoolmaster for several years, and it is quite possible that this experience contributed to his remarkable achievements as a philosopher.) Following is Wittgenstein's list:

Review the multiplicity of language-games in the following examples, and in others:

Giving orders, and obeying them
Describing the appearance of an object, or giving its measurements
Constructing an object from a description (a drawing)
Speculating about an event
Forming and testing a hypothesis
Presenting the results of an experiment in tables and diagrams
Making-up a story; and reading it
Play-acting
Singing catches
Guessing riddles
Making a joke; telling it

Solving a problem in practical arithmetic
Translating from one language into another
Asking, thanking, cursing, greeting, praying (1953, p. 11-12).

In an earlier discussion of Wittgenstein's theory of language, I once said, "All these activities involve in some way acts of saying or telling" (1960, p. 245). From this view of language as action it becomes apparent that what I have earlier described as symbolic, along with those activities that I called non-symbolic, can *all* be included within the scope of language. However, it is the intent here to draw finer distinctions and to more clearly expose the multiple dimensions of addressed meaning in contrast to those of attached meaning.

A closer inspection of the idea of "context" brings into sharper relief the clear-cut patterns and forms that language games can take; and also set the stage for a discussion of several studies of thinking that have been carried on in and through the analysis of verbal interaction. (In these studies the importance of keeping track of the *context* of what was said and done in the course of a class session was truly crucial.) The function of context in the analysis of meaning is nowhere better stated than by P. F. Strawson, who wrote:

... the context of utterance is of an importance which it is almost impossible to exaggerate; and by "context" I mean, at least, the time, the place, the situation, the identity of the speaker, the subjects which form the immediate focus of interest, and the personal histories of both the speaker and those whom he is addressing (1950, p. 336).

Conceptions of Thinking in Classroom Research

Three recent studies of thinking in the context of classroom operation will be treated here. Each investigation placed special emphasis upon the addressed mode of meaning, which is the prevalent mode of meaning represented in the teacher-student activity of the classroom. Attached meaning, however, is taken to be as basic as addressed meaning to the content of the learning tasks and materials making up the subject matters of instruction.

Each of these research projects involved extensive tape recording, and the verbatim transcription of the moment-to-moment flow of verbal interaction among teachers and students within the context of instruction, study and learning. The transcribed class sessions in all three studies were subjected to intensive analysis, with particular attention given to the relation between thinking processes and the verbal behaviors that are taken to reflect their operation. In other words, each study sought to make use of every available contextual cue that might permit inferences to be made concerning what kind of thinking was going on in the course of class discussion.

The Search for Teaching Strategies

Two of these studies explored the varieties of possible strategies that teachers might employ in fostering the development of thinking abilities in students. Both investigations began with the study of teaching "as is," without intervention of any kind, in order to determine what current practices might have to do with the development of thinking abilities, and both studies then attempted either to identify (Taba, 1963) or to formulate (Smith *et al.*, 1964) what seemed to be promising ways of developing effective teaching procedures for stimulating and training thinking.

Smith (1964) and his colleagues based their analysis of verbal interaction on a conception of thinking in terms of its logical dimensions and manifestations in behavior. A number of logical operations were identified and classified in performances assumed to represent such activities as defining, explaining, inferring, designating, classifying, evaluating, and so on. The teaching strategies sought for development were those which would equip the teacher both with effective procedures for fostering critical thinking—broadly constructed—and the ability to exercise procedures exactingly and systematically within the framework of the subject matter being studied. Teaching strategies involved combinations of "moves" (tactics?) whereby particular logical operations were either performed by the teacher in carrying on instruction, or they were structured by the teacher for performance in the sequences of verbal interaction carried on by the students. The Smith studies have been conducted in high school classrooms, grades nine through twelve, in the fields of English, social studies, mathematics, and the sciences.

Taba has also undertaken to analyze thinking processes in the classroom verbal interaction context in order to identify and develop teaching strategies. Her studies have been carried on in elementary school classrooms. As Taba says, the problem is ". . . to identify the particular teaching strategies required by particular types of learning goals, such as generating certain cognitive operations, stimulating certain types of inquiry, and integrating certain bits of information into larger concepts" (1963).

In her analysis of classroom activities, Taba has focused her observation upon the various patterns—or profiles—of instructional sequences that characterize certain styles. of teaching. These patterns, once traced, tend to reveal the manner in which the teacher paces and phases the mode of her pupils' engagement with learning content, and to indicate how the teacher may modulate and temper the thinking processes of the student by adjusting and shifting his levels of thinking appropriately to the cognitive demands of the learning task and to his present cognitive structure as a developing learner. This appears to be a most promising and realistic approach to the development of sound teaching strategies for use in elementary classrooms.

The Examination of Productive Thinking

Thinking operations and their correlates, both within and outside the classroom, were investigated by Gallagher and Aschner, with special concern for the conditions *in the classroom* under which productive thinking—self-directed and self-propelled thinking—might be found to operate (Gallagher and Aschner, 1963; Aschner, 1963). The subjects of this study included classes of homogeneously grouped gifted children in school at the junior high school level. In analyzing thought processes in terms of their productivity, Guilford's well-known "Structure of Intellect" model became the theoretical basis of procedure, with specific application of its "operations" dimension (Guilford, 1959; Guilford and Merrifield, 1960).

The formal definitions of the *operations* of intellect which became the conceptual guidelines followed in development of a classification system for categorizing thinking operations as reflective in the context of teacher-student verbal behavior interaction (Aschner, Gallagher and others, 1962) are shown below. These definitions are excerpted from the full set—including contents and products—presented by Guilford and Merrifield (1960).

Operations: Major kinds of intellectual activities or processes; things that the organism does with the raw materials of information (The authors define "information" as "that which the organism discriminates.")

Cognition: Discovery, awareness, rediscovery, or recognition of information in various forms; comprehension or understanding[1]

---

[1] In the classification system developed in the Gallagher-Aschner study, the operation, Cognition, was assimilated to the category *Cognitive-Memory*, on the grounds that evidences of cognitive operations do not show up in the context of verbal interaction, especially in the absence of kinescopic scanning of each pupil in action. It is a class of operations which we assume occurred, but which can be measured best on pencil and paper tests designed to call them forth.

Memory: Retention of information in any form

Divergent Production: Generation of information from given information where the emphasis is upon variety of output from the same source

Convergent Production: Generation of information from given information where the emphasis is upon achieving unique or conventionally accepted best outcomes

Evaluation: Reaching decisions or making judgments concerning the goodness (correctness, suitability, adequacy, desirability) of information in terms of criteria of identity, consistency, and goal satisfaction.

The transposition of Guilford's "Structure of Intellect" model into the domain of verbal behavior proved feasible and yielded reliable classifications of individual performances during class sessions in terms of the thinking either called for or expressed by teachers and/or students. Four primary operations categories were developed, each containing sub-categoried defining behaviors manifesting the primary operation in one of several ways. A fifth category, *Routine*, was constructed in which to classify all such "noncognitive" interaction behaviors as attend the daily management (M) activities of the class, and to include also certain behaviors that were seen to have possible import for the patterns of thinking operations that followed them in the class session. For example, *Verdict* (+ or − Ver) was a category used to keep track of instances in which individuals—more often teachers than students—would express praise or rebuke concerning the deportment or performance of another individual.

Some representative illustrations of the kinds of verbal performances classified according to the five primary categories of the Classification System follow:

Routine (R)
    T: That's a good job, Danny (+ Ver), or Stop that fidgeting, Harry! (− Ver)
    S: What time does the library close this afternoon? (M)

Cognitive-Memory (C-M)
    T: Who discovered the Sandwich Islands?
    S: Captain Cook. Now they're called the Hawaiian Islands.

Divergent Production (DT)[2]
    T: How many different ways can we think of for getting European

---

2 *Divergent Production* is given the symbol DT for "divergent thinking," which was the way we got to talking about this class of operations. We did not lose sight of

tourists interested in coming to the United States for vacations?

S: Well, we could meet them at the airport—or when their ships come in—with a "Welcome Wagon" full of gifts.

Convergent Production (CT)

T: Let's suppose you earn $125 a week, and by the time you get your take-home pay check, 20% of your wages has been withheld. How much actual cash would you take home?

S: Well, I think it would be just about $100.

Evaluation (ET)

T: Do you think that it is a good idea for students in junior high school to manage their own discipline problems through an honor system, maybe, or in Student Council?

S: Well, I guess so; yeah.

S: Well, if you want my honest opinion, I don't think it would work. The kids wouldn't want to squeal on each other or sentence some friend to a real tough punishment.

The Gallagher-Aschner study made no attempt to intervene or to shape teacher behavior; teachers cooperating in the study were asked to do as they normally did in their teaching activities. Some remarkable differences were found among teachers as well as students regarding the amount and occasions in which productive thinking showed itself in classroom discourse.

Among the many findings and new lines of research that this study opened up, one thing became very clear. That is, the very great service-ability of Guilford's three-dimensional model of the "Structure of Intellect," i.e., not only in terms of the observation of thinking in class-room performance, but also in relation to the *products* and *contents* dimensions for application to the construction and evaluation of instruc-tional materials. Teachers may use the S of I model as a focusing guide for the observation, analysis, interpretation and diagnosis of student behavior along its intellective dimensions. Similarly, another use of Guilford's model is seen in guiding the design and construction of in-class written work, or homework assignments that put thinking to work. The principle here (see two illustrations in the following section) involves structuring the task *for* productive thinking, by requiring initiative and self-directed dealings with the task.

---

the "productive" aspect of the operation by any means, since a central aim of the study was to identify not only the occurrence of productive thinking operations, but also the conditions and the context of their occurrence. CT is our symbol for *Convergent Production* for the same reason.

Suggestions for Teachers

A few concrete and practical suggestions for teachers have already been pointed out in the preceding section, in relation to the use of the Guilford model. This model helps teachers to become more sensitive and perceptive observers of pupil performance than may be possible in cases where teachers lack a conceptual frame of reference to deal with various ideas and problems. People sometimes forget that the teacher is both a theoretician and a practical cognitive and social psychologist. Thus in a good conceptual model is a real potential benefit.

Let me reiterate the principle, enunciated by James J. Gallagher, who said that teachers must work to provide for "flexibility within structure." This principle can be observed in the conduct of class discussion by asking for divergent, convergent, and evaluative thinking upon appropriate occasions. Further, it can be observed in the design and construction of written tasks which not only require students to apply the knowledge and understandings that they have learned, but also to engage in productive and evaluative thinking *on their own*.

Below are two in-class written tasks given to two classes of the subjects included in the Gallagher-Aschner study. In each case, the reader is invited to examine the demands of the test-task in terms of the kinds of thinking, organizing, and selecting for application that the student must undertake in carrying out its instructions.

The first written assignment was inspired by the ideas of Sir Frederic Bartlett's book called *Thinking* (1956). It represents a kind of task that calls for thinking via interpolation within a closed system. What this means is piecing together the gap in the middle of a sequential account of events in which only the beginning and the end of the "story" are available. In the "open middle" test, as some of my students have come to call it, the youngsters have studied a week-long unit on introductory bacteriology. The disease Anthrax received considerable attention both in class and in the assigned texts. These children were ninth-graders, but averaged closer to eighth-graders in age. They were given twenty minutes to study the instructions before setting to work. The two assignments which follow illustrate the basic forms or structures into which all manner of similar subject matters could be built.

Anthrax in Champaign

This is the beginning of a story: On the plains of western Nebraska a rancher grazed a herd of beef cattle on a new pasture that had lain fallow for many years. There were anthrax bacilli lying dormant on this pasture.

This is the end of that story: Three cases of anthrax were discovered in Champaign.[3] The first case was a nine-year-old boy named Jimmy. Three days after Jimmy was put under treatment for anthrax, Ed, a mechanic at a service station a few blocks away from Jimmy's home, came down with anthrax. The third case, reported five days later, was Dr. X, a dentist whose offices are located in downtown Champaign.

The middle of the story? How could the deadly disease anthrax, latent in bacilli on a pasture in Nebraska, be the original source of these three cases? That is your problem—to complete the story by filling in the gap between the beginning and the ˙end. There is no "one right answer" or "solution" to the problem. There are many possible ways in which this story could have really happened.

Instructions

Use your scientific knowledge about anthrax, your imagination, and your common sense. Make up a series of events that could have happened. Your story should stand as a believable account of how Jimmy, Ed, and Dr. X became the victims of anthrax from the plains of Nebraska. You will have........ minutes (or time) to write the "middle" of the story. Be sure to write so that the whole story fits together from beginning to end.

Read carefully. Be sure to have the "facts" in mind before you write. Head your paper with a title. You may use "Anthrax in Champaign!" or you may˙ think up a title of your own.

This task was assigned these subjects in March, the second half of their year in ninth grade. This was the third time this same group of youngsters had been tape-recorded, and the third time they had received an assignment structured so as to require self-directed productive thinking in the application of subject matter material they had earlier studied. It is clear that nearly every other kind of thinking operation is invited— required—for a first-class performance on this task.

The second assignment, presented below, was given to these same youngsters in October of the previous year. Again, they had been tape-recorded and their reading assignments investigated to see what kinds of knowledge they might fairly be expected to apply. This test was the first of its kind given to our subjects. They had just completed an introductory study of the Colonial Period in America. Notice that there is a different design or "ground plan" for this task. It represents the kind of task calling for divergent thinking in the sense of "implications" in the products dimension of Guilford's model. Students were also asked to evaluate on a fairly strict criterion, while dealing at the same time with a "contrary to fact" conditional hypothesis.

[3] Champaign, Illinois.

Teachers need not hesitate to design tests of similar kinds for their own students. It is not necessary that the youngsters be gifted for them to accomplish this kind of task. It is advisable when introducing children to tasks of this nature that the "risk level" or "test anxiety quotient" be lowered. Typically this is a novel and unfamiliar kind of assignment. The easing of tensions can be accomplished by at least two means.

First, the children should be given plenty of time to read the instructions and think out a plan of attack. Second, they should be informed, quite truthfully, that since this is a new kind of assignment that calls for a new way of thinking, they will not be graded for their performance on it. Even without grades, the classroom teacher can harvest a wealth of data about how his students use what they have studied, and the extent to which they tackle the problem with operations of thinking and imagination that may not show up regularly—if at all— on typical class subject matter quizzes and tests, achievement tests, or IQ tests. In other words, these performances are a valuable source of information for the teacher in respect to an individual child's capacities and weaknesses. They may reveal much about the child that had simply not been brought into action (or inaction) on more conventional measures.

The social studies test follows. Notice the way it structures the task —very specifically, yet requires considerable reflection and consideration of alternative possibilities and their consequences. In this test as well as the preceding one, it is perfectly clear that certain aspects of genuine problem solving and critical thinking are called for.

Let's Suppose[4]

Let's suppose that one important fact about life in our colonies had been different: *Women enjoyed the same rights and privileges as the men.* An exercise in supposing: In an essay of at least one full page in length (longer if you wish), do some supposing on the following questions. You will have .....time to think, and.....time to write.

1. *Tell what,* in your opinion, might be *two* (2) of the most important differences that equality for women would have made in the life and times of the Colonial Period.

4 Omitted time specifications in the above test and in the preceding one are not because they are classified information. It is to suggest that the teacher use his own judgment on how long students should be given to study the "specs" and how much time they should have for writing. If it were not for the risk of help from overly helpful parents, this kind of assignment could be made for overnight or even longer periods of time and lengths of performance as the teacher sees what is most appropriate for the class at the present time.

2. *Tell why,* in your judgment, each of the two differences you have decided upon would be among the *most important ones* that equality for women would have made in colonial life.

The basic design of these two assignments is in neither case specific to a given subject matter. There are almost limitless ways of adapting them to other topics and areas of the curriculum. Much care should be taken in how the test task *and* the instructions are worded. It is important to be very specific but reasonably succinct. It is wise in dealing with younger children to build in a little bit of redundance—a slight bit of repetition.

In reading children's performance on these tasks, there are many things one may look for. Did the child pick up all the cues? Did he tackle the task according to its specifications (this is not docility in meeting these kinds of stipulations)? Does he rely more on imagination and literary flair than upon what he has been asked to demonstrate that he knows from prior study? Does he break out of the framework so creatively that it is hard to decide whether the child is a rebel for rebellion's sake or so charged up with a bright idea that he takes it in hand and makes off with it? Is this child fluent? Is he laconic? Does the relation of quantity of output correlate positively or negatively with the quality of the performance? One job for the teacher here—and not necessarily in any concern for assigning a grade—is to examine the degree of "match" between the kind of thinking the child's performance reveals, and that which was programmed into and called for in the design of the assignment.

Some progress has been made toward the development of a blank-form rating sheet that could be used in assessing performances on assignments of the "open middle" design. But the only recommendation that these suggestions on task design construction merit at present is whatever "face validity" they seem to have, and the fact that they do offer the teacher a rich source of information about his student from quite a different perspective in many cases.

References

Mary Jane Aschner. "The Language of Teaching." *Teachers College Record* 61 (5): 242-52; February 1960.

Mary Jane Aschner, J. J. Gallagher and others. "A System for Classifying Thought Processes in the Context of Classroom Verbal Interaction." Urbana, Illinois: University of Illinois, Institute for Research on Exceptional Children, 1962. (Mimeographed.)

Mary Jane Aschner. "The Analysis of Verbal Interaction in the Classroom." In: *Theory and Research in Teaching*. Arno A. Bellack, editor. New York: Bureau of Publications, Teachers College, Columbia University, 1963.

Sir Frederic Bartlett. *Thinking*. New York: Basic Books, 1956.

J. S. Bruner. "On Perceptual Readiness." *Psychological Review* 64 (2); 1957.

J. J. Gallagher and Mary Jane Aschner. "A Preliminary Report on Analyses of Classroom Interaction." *Merrill-Palmer Quarterly* 9 (3): 183-94; July 1963.

J. P. Guilford. "Three Faces of Intellect." *American Psychologist* 14 (8): 469-79; August 1959.

J. P. Guilford and P. R. Merrifield. *The Structure of Intellect Model: Its Uses and Implications*. Report No. 24, from the Psychological Laboratory, The University of Southern California, Los Angeles, April 1960.

Wolfgang Köhler. *The Mentality of Apes*. New York: Harcourt, Brace & World, Inc., 1925.

B. O. Smith and others. *A Tentative Report on the Strategies of Teaching*. Urbana: University of Illinois, Bureau of Educational Research, 1964.

J. N. Spuhler, editor. *The Evolution of Man's Capacity for Culture*. Detroit: Wayne State University Press, 1959.

P. F. Strawson. "On Referring." *Mind*, July 1950. p. 336.

Hilda Taba. "Teaching Strategy and Learning." *California Journal for Instructional Improvement;* December 1963.

Ludwig Wittgenstein. *Philosophical Investigations*. Translated by G. E. M. Anscombe. New York: Macmillan Company, 1953. p. 11-12. Quoted by permission of Copyright owner, Basil Blackwell & Mott Ltd.

Motivation: Some Principles, Problems, and Classroom Applications

Thomas J. Johnson

THIS paper will attempt: (a) to present an overview of "basic" motivational theory, (b) to discuss some of the problems involved in the use of the construct, and (c) to demonstrate the application of motivational research to classroom settings.

Traditional beliefs about motivation and human behavior have sometimes led to the reification of concrete forces and structures within the human organism. Coutu (1949) illustrates the point in his "Doctrine of the Little Men":

> According to this popular theory the soul is the chief engineer; his assistant is a husky stoker called emotion who tends the fires, and, when bored, builds up a head of steam on his own initiative; we also find an aggressive stationary engineer called will who has a mind of his own, to the great annoyance and suffering of another chap called conscience, whose assistants are censors, superegos, and ids. All of these gremlins are under the general supervision of a consulting architect called reason, whose executive officer is an ego, and who is usually somewhere else when wanted. These gremlins are prolific and have large families of self-willed urges, drives, élans, entelechies, dynamisms, and autonomous motives, who are rugged individualists and self-made men. The whole tribe operates in a system of social anarchy with a legal structure of *laissez faire* and local autonomy under the slogan "free will for the gremlins." These little men are constantly getting in the way of research and socially visible (objective) thinking, and their endless quarrels and conflicts make human behavior an unpredictable enigma. The little men are fighters, constantly at war with each other, constantly blaming each other for throwing monkey wrenches into the machinery. To cover up their own delinquencies

they send the machine off on endless witch-hunting expeditions and searches for scapegoats.[1]

Having thus paid tribute and homage to the hagiology of human behavior, let us now explore some alternative conceptualizations of motivational concepts and theory.

The history of psychology is burdened with learning and/or personality theorists who have looked (sometimes with jaundiced eyes) at various aspects of the general problem of motivation. Each of these writers has attempted in somewhat different fashion to handle all or part of the total range of human beavior. As one studies the multiple variations and variegations that are manifest in these theorists, one is led to a conviction that the "theory" is essentially a personal matter. Man observes the same phenomenon from diverse points of view, and reasoning on the basis of these observations, he denotes the salient features which for him seem to be operative. Yet as for conceding that other theorists have as much in common, as much evidence to support them, as much functional value as our own, there are few who speak out boldly. Consequently, the initial task is to provide some degree of closure to the various concepts and diverse viewpoints concerning motivation.

Behavior theorists in general deal essentially with three basic concepts: (a) stimulus (S); (b) an organism (O); and (c) a response (R). These basic concepts rest in turn upon a limited number of basic assumptions. Any theory as such can be construed as an attempt (under these basic assumptions) to specify the relationships between these three basic concepts which we commonly symbolize as S-O-R. While these concepts may seem simple enough, several writers have commented on the theoretical and empirical difficulties involved in the use of the stimulus concept (e.g., Gibson, 1960), as well as the response concept (e.g., Brown, 1961). I shall not attempt to point out these difficulties, or attempt to resolve them; but the serious student is urged to examine these authors in greater detail. The primary concern at this time is to examine the basic assumptions which seem to underlie most theories of human behavior.

Basic Assumptions

Assumption 1.   *All behavior is determined.*

Perhaps this is the most insistent and pervasive assumption underlying the behavioral sciences. At a common sense level this assumption

---

[1] W. Coutu. *Emergent Human Nature.* New York: Alfred A. Knopf, Inc., 1949. p. 104.

implies that human behavior is not just a haphazard movement of muscle and limb, but presumably has some cause underlying its occurrence—some conditions which control the emergence of the responses we observe.

The child in the classroom does his homework for some cause. It may be because he is interested in getting the problems correctly answered, or because he wants to do something else which is contingent upon his completion of the assignment. It may also be because he fears the teacher, or fears the effects of the teacher's influence on his parents' behavior toward him. At any rate, the child's behavior has some "raison d'être."

Nagel (1961) has remarked on the role of the deterministic thesis in inquiry as "a regulative principle that formulates in a comprehensive way one of the major objectives of positive science, namely, the discovery of the determinants for the occurrence of events."[2] In its broadest sense the thesis implies that human behavior is lawful, and that a finite number of variables can be postulated with which we can explain human behavior. This assumption does not imply that we have already conceptualized all of the factors or variables which underlie behavior. Certainly much of human behavior appears to be "unlawful" at times. The "lawfulness" that does exist is invented or constructed by the psychologist based upon the evidence at hand, and upon the concepts which are avaliable to him. Nevertheless, underlying the thesis is a faith that, given enough time, we will be able to postulate the basic conditions which underlie all of human behavior and that we will be able to demonstrate empirically the manner in which these conditions affect human behavior.

It should be emphasized that this assumption does not necessarily deny the existence of choice by the individual in regard to the behavior in which he engages. Certainly choice can be one of the postulated conditions which control human behavior, as Tyler (1962) has noted. Many of us have chosen to be nonaggressive even though the belligerence of our adversary has previously been the occasion for aggression on our part.

Psychologists who would wish to do away with the condition or variable of choice in human behavior do so under the mistaken impression that choice and chance are equivalent terms. To know the bias of a coin is to be able to predict with greater certainty that certain events (e.g., heads) will occur more frequently.

[2] E. Nagel. *The Structure of Science.* New York: Harcourt, Brace & World, Inc., 1961. p. 605.

Assumption 2.   *Human behavior is governed by the principles of*
   (a) stimulus reduction, and (b) stimulus induction.

One experimenter investigates aggression, another creativity. One theorist uses one set of concepts, a second prefers different terminology. Empirical evidence supporting one point of view seems to contradict another point of view. Superficially there would seem to be little basis for agreement among psychologists that human behavior is governed by any general principles. Nevertheless, within contemporary psychology most theories of human behavior would seem to adhere to one of two basic principles governing the relationship between external and internal stimuli and the responses that are made.

Although there are many variant forms to the two principles, we may refer to these principles as: (a) stimulus reduction and (b) stimulus induction.

The stimulus reduction principle derives its name from the supposition that the behavior of the organism is an attempt to *reduce* or decrease the extensity or intensity of some stimuli (states or events). Tension reduction, need reduction, drive reduction, drive-stimulus reduction are a few of the more common terms which have also been used to refer to the operation of the stimulus reduction principle.

One of the earliest formulations of the principle is contained in a statement by Freud in the *Metapsychology Papers:* "The nervous system is an apparatus which has the purpose of getting rid of the stimuli that reach it, or reducing them to the lowest possible level, or which, if it were feasible, would maintain itself in an altogether unstimulated condition" (p. 63).

The principle is generally invoked to explain behavior where noxious stimulation and unpleasant consequences are involved. However, it is also used to account for behavior related to internal deficits (e.g., hunger, thirst) or vague undifferentiated need states (e.g., need for attention).

The stimulus induction principle derives its name from the supposition that the behavior of the organism represents an attempt to *increase* the extensity or intensity of some stimulus, event or state. The principle is generally invoked to help explain a wide variety of perceptual and intellectual activities which seem to result in an increase in the general or specific stimulation the organism receives (e.g., in curiosity, exploratory and orienting behaviors). The principle may also seem to underlie what Berlyne (1961) has called *ludic* behavior (play) and *epistemic* behavior (behavior which augments knowledge).

Assumption 3. *The origin of behavior is related to the existence of (a) internal stimuli (events, states),* and *(b) external stimuli. (events, states).*

Although most psychologists do not deny the existence of both internal and external stimuli, there has been considerable disagreement as to the relative importance of each in accounting for human behavior. One point of view is exemplified by Freud who conceived of the external stimuli as something which could be avoided by the organism, and hence were of minor importance. The internal events (arising out of some somatic process) could not be avoided or the organism felt tension. There is nothing inherently wrong in this approach. That is, one may assume the source of stimulation to be internal and show by what process the subsequent behavior emerges.

The real problem is to operationalize, measure, and thus verify the processes involved. However, by attributing the source of behavior to stimulation which originates within the organism, subsequent verification of the processes is almost exclusively an inferential task. Since these inferences are all to be derived from the behavior to be explained, one is thrown back on the credulity with which he accepts the basic premises. Figure 1 illustrates this viewpoint in S-O-R terms. The stimuli (S) arise within the organism (O) and the response (R) occurs.

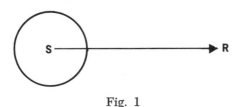

Fig. 1

A second point of view represented for the most part by earlier experimental psychologists acknowledges the existence of certain external stimuli which at birth were capable of eliciting a few differentiated responses (reflexes) and were also capable of arousing some innate response tendencies. At the same time, they acknowledged the existence of certain internal stimuli (drives) which impel the organism to action.

Like Freud, they too appear to be on solid ground. Having assumed the source of the process to be both internal and external stimuli, one may attempt to hold the internal stimuli constant and by manipulating the external stimuli observe the organism "emit" the response. Figure 2 illustrates this approach using S-O-R terms. The stimuli (S) elicit the response (R), and the organism (O) is conveniently bypassed.

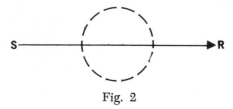

Fig. 2

However, having assumed a connection between the external stimulus and the response, it became necessary to demonstrate the chain of external and internal sequences which eventuate in the terminal response. Through inferences based upon careful, systematic observation, the behavior ultimately emitted by the organism is now generally conceptualized as a complex function involving a number of different kinds of internal stimuli or processes. These include stimuli arising from autonomic processes, stimuli arising from cognitive processes, and stimuli arising from the motor processes and the terminal response itself. As it has become necessary to invoke more and more of these internal events to explain the processes underlying behavior, the initial external stimulus itself becomes less important in governing the final response we observe. Figure 3 illustrates this conceptualization in S-O-R terms.

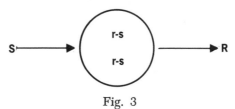

Fig. 3

The stimulus (S) enters the organism giving rise to other stimuli and responses (r-s) which eventuate in the response (R). Should additional internal events need to be posited, we may soon come to a model which bears a striking resemblance to Figure 1. However, it should be obvious that behavior theory has not come full circle. The similarity between the approaches illustrated by Figures 1 and 3 is only superficial. A requirement of any theory of human behavior is that it form a consistent whole. It should be free from *ad hoc* hypotheses, postulated whenever new facts of experience appear to be in conflict with our theory.

By introducing these concepts we can account for anything we choose, but prediction is nonexistent because we never know what additional hypotheses we will have to imagine later. In short, a critical experiment becomes impossible. Through systematic experimentation the contemporary psychologist has been able to construct and verify in part the nature of the processes within the organism which seem to be related to human behavior. As he comes to know more about these processes and the manner in which they interact, the development of more comprehensive constructs, models and theories will follow.

One such newer development in motivational theory which would seem especially applicable to teaching situations is the "Discrepancy Hypothesis" (Helson, 1948; Hebb, 1955; McClelland, 1953). This hypothesis is centered upon the contention that frequency of exposure to a particular pattern, constellation, or cluster of stimuli (states, events) will result in the organism's becoming adapted (affectively neutral) to the stimulation. In short, a person becomes accustomed to those things with which he is familiar, or which are repetitive or unchanging. Figure 4 illustrates the dynamics of the discrepancy hypothesis. Slight deviations or discrepancies from this adaptation level (AL) are hedonically or affectively positive (points B, C); large deviations or discrepancies are affectively negative (points A, D).

The hypothesis may be personally verified by immersing yourself in a tub filled with water at body temperature. Turn either the cold or hot tap and the initial sensation of change is pleasant. Empirical verification of the discrepancy hypothesis (with humans) can be found in studies by Haber (1955), Maddi (1961), and Pitts (1963). If one posits an adaptation level for difficulty or complexity of intellectual and motor tasks of the type generally found in the classroom, the generalization of this hypothesis to the classroom might reasonably follow.

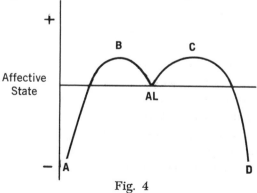

Fig. 4

From the standpoint of motivational theory, the discrepancy hypothesis offers a possible conceptual rapprochement between the empirical evidence supporting either a stimulus reduction or stimulus induction model of behavior. Whether subsequent experimentation will serve to augment this early promise is a matter of conjecture. Judging from the past history of motivational constructs some additional problems are likely to occur. One continuing source of difficulty resides in the nature of the motivation concept itself.

Nature of the Motivation Concept

In general the motive concept is derived from the observation of behavior. That is, the term motive has generally been used to refer to a class of non-observables which are antecedent to and explanatory of the particular behavior under observation. We infer the existence of the motive from our observations of these behaviors, and acknowledge the source or "cause" of the behavior to reside in some postulated state or condition. When we use the motive concept in this way, it becomes a "causal" concept. The "motive" becomes the "cause" of the behavior.

There is nothing inherently wrong with such usage. Similar inferences are made in other fields. The physicist observing a moving body in space sees it apparently change direction when in the vicinity of a larger mass, and ultimately make contact with the surface of that mass. This apparent change in direction is presumed to occur because of gravity, or in more sophisticated terms, because of the particular nature of space-time in the vicinity of matter. The physicist has postulated the existence of these conditions in order to explain the observed behavior. Similar postulations are made in other sciences as well. If we grant then that we may properly infer, postulate or construct the existence of certain states or conditions from our observation of behavior, why do we have so much difficulty in understanding motivation?

To begin with, the motive concept is nothing other than a logical extension of what the layman considers a self-evident fact, that generally speaking, common causes yield common events, common events have their origins in common causes. However obvious the validity of this premise may be in other fields, its acceptance in the realm of human behavior forces us into particular ways of viewing the phenomenon under question. If we assume that "like produces like" it becomes increasingly important to be able to denote relevant similarities and differences, on a number of different dimensions.

Certain "species" of motive in humans may be homologous in the sense that one might be able to trace out similar origins, similar goals, similar cues in the environment, similar instances or conditions under which particular motivated behavior may be said to occur. One must be careful, however, that the differences that do exist are slight, reflecting variation only in the intensity of the specific behavior. On the other hand, certain motives may be merely analogous, that is, certain behaviors may seem functionally similar, but be derived from disparate sources.

Let us briefly look at the motive concept a little more closely. We have previously stated that a motive can be considered a causal concept. All motives or motivational variables have one essential property in common, i.e., they produce or are capable of producing behavior. A group of ideas, events or objects having such a common property constitute a class. Members of the class "capable of giving rise to behavior" involve primarily motives or motivational variables. Members of the class "capable of giving rise to behavior x" involve, hopefully, a limited number of motives. Whether these motives eventuate in the specific behavior by eliciting, energizing, guiding, releasing, etc., is also important; but for our purposes we shall not be concerned with the transfer mechanisms or processes involved. What is important at this time is to recognize that when we are dealing with a cause-effect relationship, it is a *disjunctive* one.

Consider the following situation:

Frank, a fifth-grader, is observed by the teacher in the act of hitting another child. For want of a better term, let us describe this behavior as "aggressive" and attempt to postulate the motives underlying this "aggression." To rephrase the problem, what we are interested in finding are members of the class of motives "capable of giving rise to aggressive behavior."

It should become immediately obvious that a number of different motives, such as needs for attention, needs for power, feelings of hostility, etc., may be invoked, all purporting to explain the discrete behavior we have observed. What makes the class "capable of giving rise to aggressive behavior" disjunctive is (a) to see the effect, i.e., "aggressive behavior" gives no clue as to which of the presumed motives is operative; and (b) the motives themselves have little in common except that they can eventuate in "aggressive" behavior. To quote Bruner (1956): "Members of a disjunctive class exhibit defining attributes such that one or the other of these attributes can be used in identifying or categorizing them."

Although we can classify motive as a disjunctive concept, it must be emphasized that we are dealing with an extremely complex disjunctive concept at best. The fact of disjunctivity as well as the complexity have both contributed to some of the difficulty we have in understanding motivation. To illustrate, we shall attempt to differentiate some of the more important factors contributing to this complexity.

We have already remarked on one of these factors. *A discrete behavior may occur through any one of a number of different motives.* As can be seen by Figure 5, any of the three motives is capable of producing the response R_x. To observe the behavior affords no insight into which motive is functional.

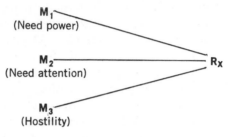

Fig. 5

A second factor contributing to the complexity of our concept is that *any one motive may give rise to any one of a number of different behaviors.* Figure 6 provides an illustration of this factor. To know the motive gives us no insight into which behavior will occur. An individual with needs for attention, for example, may be observed in a wide range of behaviors ranging from aggression to crying to autism. The existence of such inconsistency places some constraints on the predictive power of the concept.

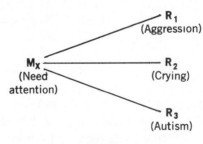

Fig. 6

To further complicate the concept, a third factor also must be acknowledged. *The motive itself may be operating, but no relevant overt response occurs.* The individual who is fasting is surely hungry; yet we can observe no food-taking on his part. While we may want to introduce "individual choice" as a contributing condition in this case, nevertheless, the hunger "motive" has not produced its customary response.

M_1_____ No observed response

(Hunger)

Fig. 7

Bruner (1956) has previously remarked on some of the strategies for dealing with disjunctive concepts. While his subjects used a number of different strategies, they tended to focus on attempts to select attributes which are common to members of the class or which occur in the majority of the members of a class. Essentially, these strategies can be construed as attempts to make the disjunctive concept more conjunctive.

Within psychology the primary method used to make the motive concept more conjunctive has been through classification, utilizing some existing commonalities, or employing arbitrary classification schemes to produce a similar effect. If we examine these classification systems in terms of the "causal" nature of the motive concept, they can be reduced to three main types: (a) classification according to cause; (b) classification according to effect; (c) classification according to cause-effect. We shall discuss each of these briefly.

Classification According to Cause

In order to use a classification system which focuses on causes only, it is necessary to assume either that the effects themselves are of equal hierarchical value, or that they have no salient discriminable differences, or that they are unimportant. Historically, some of the earliest attempts at a classification scheme based on causes concerned themselves with the nature and relationships between various types of causes—formal, final, efficient, etc. The major focus of this kind of attempt was to shed insight into the nature of the concept of causality, however; and it assumed that the effects themselves were unimportant. Since the psychologist is primarily interested in human behavior, i.e., effects, such an assumption seems untenable. Hence, he must attempt a different method if classifying by causes is to be functional.

It would be possible to postulate a different cause for every effect, except that human behavior appears to manifest itself in so many varied forms that such a system would seem to defeat itself by its own weight. The only remaining possibility of using a causal basis for classifying is to postulate a master cause for all effects. Surprisingly, a wide range of contemporary personality theories still invoke master motive concepts related to vitalism, finalism, aristogenesis, holism, self-realization, and self-actualization. Unfortunately, with the possible exception of Rogers (1954), few of the theorists who espouse these points of view offer sufficient empirical evidence to support their positions. They apparently view the phenomenon of human behavior with the unreasoning wonder of a child and assume that behavior happens because it was meant to happen. Although conceptualizations of this type have enjoyed some degree of popularity within education in the past, they appear to be losing ground to the more explicit models afforded by the other classification systems.

Classification According to Effect

In order to use a causal classification system focused upon the effects, it is necessary to classify the effects first, and then to postulate a single cause or a reduced number of causes of any class of effects. The early "trait" theorists essentially used this method. Important human behaviors were first delineated, and then a biological or internal basis or source was postulated to account for the given class of behaviors. *Gregarious* people (class of effects) are *gregarious* (effect) because they are naturally *gregarious* (cause). In its simplest form, this type of classification scheme can lend to some problems of circularity, as the previous example illustrates. However, as this scheme has been used by most behavior theorists, more rigorous logical restraints have been imposed (e.g., McClelland, 1953; Maslow, 1954).

In Maslow's theory of motives, human behavior is taxonomized along a hierarchical social-desirability continuum which ranges from primitive biological cravings (e.g., hunger, thirst) to the "crave of beauty." Underlying behavior at each level then are the appropriate needs: physiological, safety, belongingness, love, esteem, self-actualization, understanding, and aesthetic. The strength of this method of classification is also its weakness. By remaining at a general level and dealing with a generalized concept of motive, we can greatly simplify human behavior, but by using a general motive concept we also lessen the ability to make *specific* predictions concerning the individual and his behavior.

Classification According to Cause-Effect

This method of classification involves classifying *both* the external and internal conditions under which the effect occurs, as well as the effect itself. Simply stated, this entails careful specification of the external and internal stimuli (S and s) as well as specification of overt and covert responses (R and r). Contemporary theories which seem to use this scheme would include those based on a reinforcement model (Skinner, 1953) or a neurophysiological model (e.g., Hebb, 1955) as well as those who invoke cognitive and affective mediational processes to account for a wide range of human behavior (e.g., Mowrer, 1960 a, b).

The obvious advantage of the cause-effect method of classification is that it facilitates the development of motivational theories which can predict *specific* human behavior as well as explain why it occurs. It seems to be axiomatic in science that predictive power increases as there is greater specification of the conditions which govern the occurrence of a phenomenon. And because this method requires a strong empirical foundation, it would seem to have the most conceptual promise. However, it should be recognized that the translation and practical application to the classroom of any of these models should be done not only at the conceptual level, but at the operational level as well. As an illustration, let me review two recent investigations on classroom motivation.

Pupil Motives and Traits

The first of these studies attempted to look at pupil personality, using the McClelland (1951) concepts of motive, trait, and schema. In McClelland's theory, *motive* refers to the satisfactions sought by the individual. *Trait* refers to the learned habits or customary responses of the individual. *Schema* refers to the individual's conception of the world. The investigation attempted to examine the relationship between (a) students' motives; (b) the traits they manifest in the classroom; and (c) one aspect of schema—pupil expectations for teacher-leader behavior.

Subjects were 167 girls and 208 boys with normal age-grade placement in sixth to eleventh grade classes. The community could be described as lower middle-class with almost all of the parents being semiskilled or skilled tradesmen, minor office employees, and small businessmen.

Schema: Smith's (1960) adaptation of the Ohio State *Leader Behavior Description Questionnaire* (LBDQ) was prepared for use in the classroom using two dimensions: expectations for initiating structure, and expectations for consideration.[3] The correlation between these two sets of expectations is .19.

Motives: Four TAT type pictures were presented as a group test using standard procedure. Scoring was done on the presence or absence of imagery related to the three motives employed in the study: *n ach, n aff,* and *n pow.* The scorers checked their interpretations against the "expert" interpretation presented in Atkinson (1958). Using the Atkinson formula, interjudge reliabilities ranged from .81 - .95. Each subject was assigned three separate motive scores ranging from 0 to 4 based on the number of stories which contained achievement, power, or affiliation imagery. Low, moderate, and high motive groups were then formed, corresponding to scores of zero, one, or two plus on a particular motive.

Traits: Sociometric data are typically used as operational definitions of sentiment or interaction. We conceived the choices, best friend, best student (achieving), and most influential (get the other children to do what they wanted) as essentially veridical perceptions by the observer concerning habits, or families of habits, which the observed either typically manifests or manifests at crucial times, each child suggesting three or four children who fit a description and three or four who did not. Each choice was weighted and summed. Because different size classes were involved, a distribution of scores for each class was determined and then divided arbitrarily at the first and third quartiles. Individuals were then placed into one of three trait groups: Low (Q_1 and below), Moderate ($Q_2 + Q_3$), and High (Q_4) depending on the relevant trait.

Figure 8 shows the plot of mean expectations for (a) *consideration* as a function of three levels of affiliation motive and trait; and (b) *initiating structure* as a function of two levels of achievement motive and three levels of achievement trait. Separate analyses of variance showed a significant main effect of affiliation motivation on expectations for consideration ($F = 3.33$, df $= 2/366$, p $< .05$) and fairly strong effects for both achievement motive ($F = 3.60$, df $= 1/369$, p $< .06$) and trait ($F = 3.06$, df $= 2/369$, p $< .05$) and expectations for initiating structure. Intercorrelations between the three motives were low ($- .13$ to $+ .07$).

[3] *Initiating structure* refers to teacher-leader behavior which involves task accomplishment through setting deadlines, organizing work procedures, and insisting on good work. *Consideration* refers to teacher-leader behavior which facilitates interpersonal satisfactions in the group through being friendly, listening to pupils' suggestions, and taking pupils' wishes into account when decisions are made. (Sometimes referred to as "deskside manner.")

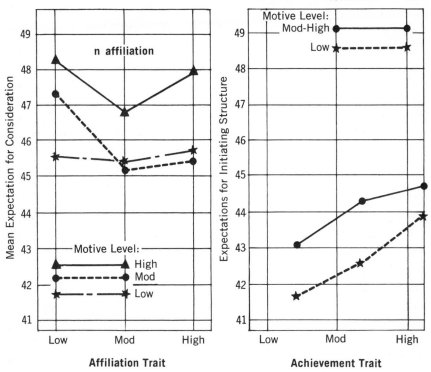

Fig. 8. Mean expectation for (a) *consideration* as a function of affiliation motive and trait and (b) *initiating structure* as a function of achievement motive and trait.

These results would seem clearly to indicate that children have differential expectations for teacher-leader behavior based in part upon their individual motive structure and their success in achieving satisfaction through relevant instrumental activities. More interestingly, the data *imply* that what the teacher does in the classroom, his characteristic behavior, can have important, predictable effects on pupil motivation and behavior.

If a teacher's behavior were generally high on consideration, and low on initiating structure, the level of satisfaction among children with affiliation needs would tend to be optimal, and reciprocal affiliative behaviors on their part would tend to increase. On the other hand, among students with achievement needs, not only might the level of satisfaction tend to be lower, but achievement behavior itself would tend to decrease. Such an outcome could have some obvious consequences for teacher-pupil interaction and the teaching-learning process.

The Teacher's Perception of Causation

The second study to be discussed here was designed to explore some rather fundamental questions about motivation in the classroom. What are the cues (from a child's behavior) which form the basis for teachers' inferences of motivation or other "causes" underlying a child's behavior? How is a teacher's subsequent behavior toward a child influenced by his perceptions of what guides, directs, or causes the child's behavior? The basic problem was to investigate some of the determinants and consequences of the teacher's perception of causation.

The theory and methodology underlying the study are explained in greater detail elsewhere (Johnson, Feigenbaum, and Weiby, 1964), but the basic experimental framework proceeded in the following manner:

Phase I. Female Ss attempted to teach an arithmetic unit (multiplying by 10's) to two fourth grade boys A and B (actually fictitious) who were in another room. After S had presented the concept, the "students" supposedly worked on problems based on the concept. After a short period of time E returned with a previously prepared work sheet purporting to be B's work up to that point, and S was allowed to talk to B briefly via a one-way intercom system. E later returned with all of A's work and the rest of B's work on the task. S was permitted to talk briefly to A, and the first experimental questionnaire was administered.

Phase II. Ss were then given two "fictitious" cumulative folders containing the personal histories of A and B. Ss familiarized themselves with these data and then attempted to teach a second unit (multiplying by 20's), after which the students again worked related problems. After a period of time Ss were asked whose work they would like to see and were allowed to talk with that student. This choice was made again at the end of the task and Ss communicated briefly with their choice. The second questionnaire was then administered, a plausible (but irrelevant) purpose was explained, and the experiment was terminated.

The experiment was designed to permit variation of (a) B's performance on an initial task (low), (b) information concerning B's task-relevant characteristics (positive or negative), and (c) B's performance on a second task (high or low). Throughout the experiment A was constant on performance (high) and characteristics (positive). Table 1 depicts the overall design which involved four groups of 20 Ss each.

Experimental Groups

	Neg Lo	Neg Hi	Pos Lo	Pos Hi
B's performance				
1st task	Low	Low	Low	Low
Questionnaire Y₁				
B's characteristics	Neg	Neg	Pos	Pos
B's performance	Low	High	Low	High
2nd task				
Questionnaire Y₂				

Table 1. Experimental Design

Two results are especially applicable to this discussion. Our findings indicate that if a pupil does poorly on a task (student B), teachers will tend to perceive the cause of this performance as internal to the student and attribute negative characteristics to him (low IQ, low social class, troublesome). If he does well (student A), they attribute positive characteristics. However, when students who have done poorly in the past improve in their performance (Pos Hi, Neg Hi), teachers tend either to perceive themselves as responsible ("I got after him," "I did a better job.") or to perceive other external causes ("He copied from A," "He cheated."). In light of these findings, it is not surprising that classroom teachers should acknowledge "motivating" students to be their most important problem.

Although a growing number of writers have commented on the need to relate pure and applied research and to validate the principles developed in the laboratory to real life situations (e.g., Festinger, 1953; French, 1953; Hilgard, 1956), their admonishments are frequently overlooked. An important methodological consideration in the previous investigation was the use of a simulated teaching situation to manipulate the independent variables of interest. While the particular strategy of simulation employed in this study involved a teacher-pupil triad, alternative types of teaching-learning situations seem equally amenable to controlled experimentation using the simulation format. One obvious advantage to this type of research lies in its easy generalization to the real life classroom.

Earlier it was suggested that the application of motivational theory to the classroom should be made at the operational as well as the conceptual level. Thus it appears unlikely that popular constructs such as needs for attention and drives (e.g., hunger, sex) are particularly useful to the classroom teacher. If the teacher is to influence and change the behavior of his pupils, he must either capitalize on the child's existing motive structure or use motivational techniques which are amenable to his control in the classroom setting.

These latter techniques would include: (a) techniques based upon the social system of the classroom (e.g., competition, cooperation, group sanctions); (b) techniques based upon the fate control he exercises (e.g., reward, punishment); and (c) techniques based upon the task or activity to be completed (e.g., solubility of problems). Research and theory which clarify the relationship between variables of this character and pupil performance would seem to offer most promise for development of viable motivational strategies. The need is manifest, but the quest is not an easy one.

Bibliography

J. W. Atkinson. *Motives in Fantasy, Action, and Society.* New York: D. Van Nostrand Co., Inc., 1958.

D. E. Berlyne. *Conflict, Arousal, and Curiosity.* New York: McGraw-Hill Book Company, Inc., 1960.

J. S. Brown. *The Motivation of Behavior.* New York: McGraw-Hill Book Company, Inc., 1961.

J. Bruner, Jacqueline J. Goodnow and G. Austin. *A Study of Thinking.* New York: Science Editions, 1962.

W. Coutu. *Emergent Human Nature.* New York: Alfred A. Knopf, Inc., 1949.

L. Festinger, S. Schachter and K. Back. "The Operation of Group Standards." In: D. Cartwright and A. Zander, editors. *Group Dynamics: Research and Theory.* Evanston: Row, Peterson & Co., 1953. p. 204-22.

J. R. P. French and L. Coch. "Overcoming Resistance to Change." In: D. Cartwright and A. Zander, editors. *Group Dynamics: Research and Theory.* Evanston: Row, Peterson & Co., 1953. p. 257-79.

S. Freud. "Triebe und Triebschicksale." *Inter. Z. f. arztl. Psychoanal.* 3:84-100; 1915. ["Instincts and their vicissitudes." In: S. Freud, *Collected Papers,* Vol. IV, London: Hogarth, 1925.]

J. J. Gibson. "The Concept of the Stimulus in Psychology." *American Psychologist* 15: 694-703; 1960.

R. N. Haber. "Discrepancy from Adaptation Level as a Source of Affect." *Journal of Experimental Psychology* 56: 370-75; 1958.

D. O. Hebb. "Drives and the C.N.S." [conceptual nervous system]. *Psychological Review* 62: 243-54; 1955.

H. Helson. "Adaptation Level as a Basis for a Quantitative Theory of Frames of Reference." *Psychological Review* 55: 297-313; 1948.

E. Hilgard. *Theories of Learning.* Second edition. New York: Appleton-Century-Crofts, Inc., 1956.

T. J. Johnson, Rhoda Feigenbaum and Marcia Weiby. "Some Determinants and Consequences of the Teacher's Perception of Causation." *Journal of Educational Psychology* 55: 237-46; 1964.

S. Maddi. "Affective Tone During Environmental Regularity and Change." *Journal of Abnormal and Social Psychology* 62: 338-45; 1961.

D. C. McClelland. *Personality.* New York: Dryden Press, 1951.

D. C. McClelland, J. W. Atkinson, R. A. Clark and E. L. Lowell. *The Achievement Motive.* New York: Appleton-Century-Crofts, Inc., 1953.

A. H. Maslow. *Motivation and Personality.* New York: Harper & Row, Inc., 1954.

O. H. Mowrer. *Learning Theory and Behavior.* New York: John Wiley & Sons, Inc., 1960a.

O. H. Mowrer. *Learning and Symbolic Processes.* New York: John Wiley & Sons, Inc., 1960b.

E. Nagel. *The Structure of Science.* New York: Harcourt, Brace & World, Inc., 1961.

C. Pitts. Personal communication.

C. R. Rogers and Rosalind F. Dymond, editors. *Psychotherapy and Personality Change.* Chicago: University of Chicago Press, 1954.

B. F. Skinner. *Science and Human Behavior.* New York: Macmillan Company, 1953.

L. M. Smith. *Pupil Expectations of Teacher Leadership Behavior.* Unpublished Final Report. U.S. Office of Education Cooperative Research Project No. 570 (8183), 1960.

Leona E. Tyler. "Toward a Workable Psychology of Individuality." In: Judy Rosenblith and W. Allinsmith, editors. *The Causes of Behavior.* Boston: Allyn and Bacon, 1962.

ASCD Publications

YEARBOOKS

Balance in the Curriculum Raises questions and issues affecting balance in instruction $4.00

Fostering Mental Health in our Schools Relates mental health to the growth and development of children and youth in school _____ 3.00

Guidance in the Curriculum Treats that part of guidance which can and should be done by teachers _____ 3.75

Individualizing Instruction Seeks to identify and enhance human potential _____ 4.00

Leadership for Improving Instruction Illustrates leadership role of persons responsible for improving instruction _____ 3.75

Learning and Mental Health in the School Examines school's role in enhancing competence and self-actualization of pupils _____ 5.00

Learning and the Teacher Analyzes classroom practices, seeking to derive ideas and concepts about learning _____ 3.75

Look at Continuity in the School Program, A Studies articulation problems, kindergarten through high school _____ 4.00

New Insights and the Curriculum Projects and examines new ideas in seven frontier areas _____ 5.00

Peceiving, Behaving, Becoming: A New Focus for Educaton Applies new psychological insights in education ____ 4.50

Research for Curriculum Improvement Helps teachers and others carry on successful research in school or classroom _____ 4.00

Role of Supervisor and Curriculum Director _____ 4.50

What Shall the High Schools Teach? Raises questions related to content of the instructional program in secondary schools _____ 3.75

PAMPHLETS

Assessing and Using Curriculum Content $1.00	Junior High School We Saw, The _____ $1.50
Better Than Rating _____ 1.25	Juvenile Delinquency _____ 1.00
Changing Curriculum Content _____ 1.00	Language and Meaning _____ 2.75
Children's Social Learning _____ 1.75	Learning More About Learning _____ 1.00
Curriculum Change: Direction and	Matter of Fences, A _____ 1.00
Process _____ 2.00	New Curriculum Developments _____ 1.75
Curriculum Materials 1966 _____ 1.25	New Dimensions in Learning _____ 1.50
Discipline for Today's Children and	Nurturing Individual Potential _____ 1.50
Youth _____ 1.00	Personalized Supervision _____ 1.75
Elementary School Science _____ 1.00	Self-Contained Classroom, The _____ 1.25
Elementary School We Need, The ____ 1.25	Strategy for Curriculum Change _____ 1.25
Extending the School Year _____ 1.25	Supervision in Action _____ 1.25
Foreign Language Teaching in Elemen-	Teaching Music in the Elementary
tary Schools _____ 1.00	School: Opinion and Comment ____ 1.25
Freeing Capacity To Learn _____ 1.00	Theories of Instruction _____ 2.00
High School We Need, The _____ .50	Three R's in the Elementary School ___ 1.50
Human Variability and Learning _____ 1.50	What Are the Sources of the
Improving Language Arts Instruction	Curriculum? _____ 1.50
Through Research _____ 2.75	What Does Research Say About
Intellectual Development: Another Look 1.75	Arithmetic? _____ 1.00
Junior High School We Need, The ____ 1.00	Child Growth Chart _____ .25

Discounts on quantity orders of same title to single address: 2-9 copies, 10%; 10 or more copies, 20%. Orders for $2 or less must be accompanied by remittance. Postage and handling will be charged on all orders not accompanied by payment.

ASCD membership dues, including Yearbook and subscription to EDUCATIONAL LEADERSHIP, official journal of the Association—$10.00. Subscriptions only—$5.50 (included in both regular and comprehensive membership dues). Comprehensive membership (includes all ASCD publications issued during the 12-month membership period)—$15.00.

Order from:

Association for Supervision and Curriculum Development, NEA
1201 Sixteenth Street, N.W., Washington, D.C. 20036